LIBRARY

1216 SUNBURY RD.
COLUMBUS, OHIO

Remembering How We Stood

Remembering
How We Stood

Bohemian Dublin at the Mid-Century

John Ryan

Taplinger

First published in the United States in 1975 by
TAPLINGER PUBLISHING CO., INC.
New York, New York

Second Printing

Copyright © 1975 by John Ryan

All rights reserved

Printed in the Republic of Ireland

820.99415
R988r
1975

Library of Congress Catalog Card Number: 75-8412

ISBN 0-8008-6770-x

For Dee

But it won't be always summer—not for us; there are bad times
coming
When you and I will look with envy on old photographs,
Remembering how we stood. . . .

Valentin Iremonger : ' Clear View in Summer '
from *Reservations*

Acknowledgments

The author wishes to thank the following for permission to use certain extracts used in this work: Oliver D. Gogarty S.C. for a quotation from a poem of his father's; Mrs Evelyn O'Nolan for a quotation from Brian O'Nolan's *The Third Policeman*; Mrs Patrick Kavanagh for two excerpts from a poem by Patrick Kavanagh and The Bodley Head for an excerpt from James Joyce's *Ulysses*.

Contents

Introduction

These reminiscences, or memoirs (for what follows is neither biography nor autobiography) are concerned with the people whom I knew in Dublin at about the middle of the century, when I was a young and (I suspect) callow fellow.

The period 1945-1955, for the arts in Ireland, was a particularly rich one—considering the golden age that had preceded, and remembering the death of both Yeats and Joyce, and the moratorium in letters that would, most thought, predictably follow. But many factors conspired to make the new decade the prolific one that it turned out to be, and not the least of these was a universal reaction following the insularity of the five wartime years of neutrality. The windows had been flung open and, intellectually speaking, people were breathing again.

Many writers who later became internationally known, such as Edna O'Brien, J.P. Donleavy and Brendan Behan, were then being seduced into taking their first tremulous steps in literature in the half-hostile obscurity of Dublin. Others, like Patrick Kavanagh and Myles na gCopaleen, still young men, who were denied the wider acclaim which would have been theirs but for World War II, were making a delayed debut—late starters, like many others. Much happened in that short span, but there was little cohesion or plan, so that it would be too much to claim that anything like a literary movement was born—except in the sense that AE defined literary movements: 'five or six people who live in the same town and hate each other cordially.' Yet it is possible that history may disagree; she may find so many unlabelled loose ends lying around but belonging to the same period, excessive and untidy, and call it the post-Yeatsian or the Literary Skinhead Age, whereupon all the disparate elements that gave the time its special flavour will be made to fall in beneath one unifying academic banner.

Those I knew and liked the most, and whom it is my present ambition to recall, were linked together by bonds of time, location and circumstance—but not invariably by those of artistic purpose, mutual admiration or even friendship. And yet, in a peculiar Dublin way there did exist a rough-and-ready *camaraderie* that was only from time to time maimed by exceptionally gross infidelities and which was the outcome of a mutual history of chronic impecuniosity, the abuse of nonentities, the usual grey savageries inflicted by the establishment on the artist, but mostly the common experience of neglect— financial and critical.

But all these things could be, and were, occasionally ameliorated by a good laugh, a charitable act, a kind thought or, better again, a ball of malt. What is clear to me as I look back is that no more singular a body of characters will ever rub shoulders again at any given time, or a city so uniquely bizarre as ' literary ' Dublin then was, will evermore be seen. Because of this and because I happened to be so strategically placed (*in media res*—as it were), I finally yielded to a persistent temptation to set down on paper these recollections while they were still comparatively green; before they yellowed, became arid and were ultimately, like lost memories, borne away on the wind of time but, above all in the words of an old friend and colleague of those days, the poet Valentin Iremonger, ' lest the wrong story fan out into history.'

John Ryan
Dublin, 1974

PART ONE

The Time and the Place

The shadow of a flying bird speeds away with the bird, but the shadow of a friend abides long after the friend has gone out of our lives . . .

George Moore : *Hail and Farewell*

Ireland wasn't golden always, but it was golden sometimes and in 1950 it was, all in all, a golden age for me and for others.

Harold Pinter : *Mac* (1968)

The Fair City

To take an active part in the artistic life of any small city is as cuddlesome a thing as to immerse oneself in a hip-bath of piranha fish. But before we now take that vicarious plunge let us first take a look at the bath.

A visiting Englishman, John Head, writing in the year 1600, had this to say about Dublin:

> Many of its inhabitants call this city Divlin, quasi Divel's Inn, and very properly it is by them so termed; for there is hardly in the world a city that entertains such devil's imps as that doth. If any knavishly break, murder, rob or are desirous of polygamy, they straightforward repair thither.

Sir Jonah Barrington in his *Recollections* (1835) saw it more for itself than its denizens:

> Dublin, the second city in the British Empire, though it yields in extent, yields not in architectural beauty to the metropolis of England.

It has been called many things since then, including dear, old and dirty; but to most of those who feel deeply about the place, it is ' the fair city '.

It is a writers' city—or at least a city more written about than any other of its size that I can think of. It was and is a city of many authors—from Swift to Beckett. Around Saint Patrick's Cathedral there are vestiges of the Dean's Dublin still to be seen, and there is much of the Dublin of George Bernard Shaw's boyhood extant today. Particular districts bring others to mind : elegant Merrion Square reminds us of Oscar Wilde's elegant upbringing, while the hauteur of Ely Place proclaims that both George Moore and Oliver St John Gogarty lived in it; even though the residence of the first—as fine a Georgian city house as there is, confronted the rather charming Victorian confection on the opposite side of the street belonging to the second—put one in mind of Eliza Doolittle being presented to Mrs FitzHerbert.

Rathgar, clad in its reddish-brown brick, like an old russet apple or a lingering autumnal evening, is William Carleton and AE and the first years of James Joyce. There is still much of O'Casey's world to be seen, heard and felt in the north city and if many old tenements have made way for corporation flats, it is very much a case of *plus ça change, plus c'est la même chose.* There is Yeats's Sandymount and Rathfarnham; Brendan Behan's Royal Canal (along which was heard the ' Ould Triangle ') and Patrick Kavanagh's Grand Canal (' leafy with love banks ')—so near yet so many light years apart . . . Myles na gCopaleen's, James Stephens's, L.A.G. Strong's, J.P. Donleavy's—so many Dublins overlapping and interlacing, replacing and embracing.

But the place itself is older than its own memories or historians' guesses. Ptolemy gives it prominence in his atlas of the world in 140 A.D., calling it Eblana—a name that is commemorated in one of the city's theatres. We now use the Irish word Dubhlinn (the dark pool) a name that belonged more to the Danish occupation of the city (from the eighth to the eleventh century) rather than the earlier form, Baile Atha Cliath (the town of the ford of the hurdles) although we (rather perversely) use this form when we are speaking Irish.

The ancient name of her river Liffey is Anna Livia and once, a long time ago, a man must have tarried by her banks. He had a plan. Instead of crossing the rickety structure of wattles which formed a rough viaduct over the shallows at this spot, he decided to guard the ford and to extract tribute from those who needed to use it. It had strategic importance as it straddled

one of the roads to the royal capital at Tara. Oliver St John
Gogarty in later days, from a bridge on the river, evoked the
primordial scene when, with a

> *. . . longing for the taintless air,*
> *I called that desolation back again,*
> *Which reigned when Liffey's widening banks were bare;*
> *Before Ben Edair gazed upon the Dane,*
> *Before the hurdle ford, and long before*
> *Finn drowned the young men by its meadowy shore.*

In a short time other dwellings grew on, or clustered about,
his original structure, and I'll wager the first was an inn, the
second a blacksmith, the third a wheelwright, and the fourth
a brothel. No offence intended, but in 1917 (admittedly the
city had a British garrison) there were in Dublin 132 known
brothels and 1,700 street girls. A lady unless she was accompanied by a man would not dare to venture down the General
Post Office side of O'Connell Street.

In the fulness of time (and there was plenty of it, God having
created an abundance thereof) this unlawful assembly, this
squattage, this random grouping, became a village which, in
turn, expanded to the importance of a town or borough; only
when this became the seat of a bishop did it attain to the
eminence of being a city. Dublin, because of her two cathedrals
—St Patrick's and Christ Church—each possessing the coveted
throne or ' cathedra '—has owned this status for nearly eight
centuries, although her population in a census of 1659 was
under nine thousand, much of it living outside the walls.
Strangely, Dublin never was, despite all this, the ecclesiastical
capital—an honour given to, and retained by, Armagh.

With a population of just over a half million, Dublin by my
time was the same in size as Samuel Pepys' London. It, too,
was a capital city, the seat of government, administration, law
and learning. Already, like London, it had spawned a considerable civil service, with all the bureaucratic appurtenances
thereof, as well as housing the diplomatic representatives of
many nations within its gates. It was also the busiest seaport

and the focal point of industry and commerce. It was a city by any estimate, but was yet within the limits of the human scale —though only just.

It was a city still happily tailored to the requirements of man. The ambulatory Dubliner found it well within his stamina to walk most of the important central streets during the course of his long day. He was on speaking terms with almost everybody in his own sphere of activities and on nodding terms with the rest. In the placid, traffic-free boulevards he could dally and browse; for time was still on his side; but mostly he could exchange news and views, relay gossip and disseminate scandal. Like Pepys' London, bolder, more pushing citizens could (and did) poke their noses into the very administration, and their fingers into every pie—City Hall and Dublin Castle being much the same thing to them as Whitehall and 'Change were to the ambitious Pepys.

The war had 'frozen' all building and public works. Time, in that sense, had stopped in the summer of 1939. It might have been 1839 but for the fact that there had been some development in the preceding decade, though this was mainly outward and suburban. A huge red-tiled dormitory city (not to be confused with the lost 'nighttown' of Joyce), Crumlin, had been built, partly to house the expanding population and partly to re-house the denizens of those faded glories, the Georgian town houses of the rich, long since turned into teeming, squalid tenements. Brendan Behan, himself one of a family of such refugees, resettled in this hinterland, remembered how his father had got a 'bad turn' on looking out a window on the first morning in his new corporation house and seeing an open field complete with a cow!

Dublin central, the O'Connell Street area in particular had been devastated in the 1916 rising, and later during the civil war of the 'twenties. It was about as much as her dazed citizens could do, pulling themselves up from the rubble (by their own shoe-laces) physically to replace what had been lost, without bothering excessively about architectural niceties, in the following two frenetic decades that included fratricidal strife, the Wall Street crash and the 'economic' war. It is a poor thing, this O'Connell Street, with an occasional exception like the Gresham Hotel (which has at least period grace like a Cunard liner of the mid-thirties), but it is our own. For the rest, the thoroughfare is 'soda-fountain' modern—out of Barbara Hutton by Walter Gropius.

Architecturally, Dublin was a Georgian city with all the aesthetic coherence that this implies; even the Victorian speculators came to terms, in their own way, with this concept so that it was only in the most recent times that developments wholly alien to the eighteenth-century ideal were pile-driven and implanted on the original Georgian matrix.

It was in many respects the city that Joyce had left behind. True, there had been a growth in population in these forty-odd years since his departure—a gradual, barely perceptible growth, yet one which had managed to erode stealthily the open commons, small green fields, groves, culverts and many a leafy lovers' lane that stood between the old city and her attendant villages of Howth, Clontarf, Cabra, Drumcondra, Kilmainham, Clondalkin, Rathfarnham, Dundrum, Sandymount, Blackrock, Kingstown and Dalkey. But the concrete had not yet seeped through every nook and cranny of what was metropolitan Dublin and her four companion boroughs.

Since his day, the most significant change has been a psychological rather than a physical one; the Dublin of a half-century earlier was already a faded eighteenth-century beauty in greatly reduced circumstances (though, even in poverty, gracious)—her hour as second city of the Empire had long passed. The Act of Union and the subsequent departure from her purlieus of the sham-squires, the bankrupt baronets, the rakes of Mallow and the rest of the motley assembly of settlers and adventurers that made up the 'gintry', their few grubby shillings of Castlereagh's blood-money in their breeches pocket, had left her empty and penniless. These vanished carpet-baggers were Dublin's tragi-comic version of the Flight of the Earls.

This bathos was regularly commemorated by W. H. Conn, the black-and-white artist, in his numerous pen sketches in the now defunct *Dublin Opinion* (a humorous monthly), showing their crinolined and peruked ghosts descending from ethereal sedan-chairs outside real Georgian doorways, while time solid, bare-footed, twentieth-century urchins and street-arabs disported themselves on swings improvized between neo-classical pillars or played on the gracious, winding stairs, beneath richly stuccoed ceilings and Angelica Kaufmann medallions.

This then was substantially the same city that continued to stand or, with occasional lapses, fall around us; in other words, Joyce's physical city but with motor cars (few and far between) and neon-lighting (switched off for the ' emergency ').

It was, in 1943 (the first year of my adult association with it), an enormous town on the brink of becoming a city. As a setting it was big enough (which is to say, sufficiently un-provincial) for the larger-than-life egos of those whom we are about to meet, but not so much so as to drown them.

Those of us who live that long are likely to see, by the end of this century, a city that will stretch from Drogheda in the north to the town of Wicklow in the south and as far west as Naas. God knows how many it will be trying to contain, but it should be as densely packed and contain as much charm as Glasgow. Already Dublin is breaking itself up into self-suffi-cient zones and groupings while the centre atrophies and dies —and thus a city dies.

How much will the sense of belonging to one large, even if disputatious, family also have died by then?

2

O What a Lovely Emergency!
(1939—1945)

Ye shall hear of wars and rumours of wars.
St Matthew (24 : 6)

C'est magnifique, mais ce n'est pas la guerre.
Maréchal Bosquet (In reference to the
Charge of the Light Brigade)

The ' Emergency ' (God bless us), was a piece of word fright-fulness of our own invention. Young as we were as a nation and new as the forms of government were to us then, we lagged behind none in the opaqueness of our officialese. The ' Emergency ' as a description of this sanguine holocaust calls for a new noun to replace ' euphemism '. But there you are; we were obliged to refer to the war thus mildly.

Semantics aside, the country itself, however, was on a real war footing. The volunteer army was, if anything, over-manned, posing a problem almost beyond the physical or technical resources of the army headquarters staff to feed and house it. In addition, there was a considerable ' home guard ' which was, in effect, a first line reserve. These hosts might only be referred to in print as the ' Defence Forces '. Paddy Kavanagh did not endear himself to many by suggesting that these would be hard put to defend a field of potatoes against an invasion of crows.

He was wrong. The allies seriously considered invading the state in 1943 but were dissuaded only by the realization that, however inevitable the outcome, there would be a frightful welter of blood before this goal was achieved. The morale of the Irish army was unquestionable; it is no exaggeration that they were determined to fight it out to the finish, and that many volunteers had chosen the Irish army rather than the British one because they genuinely believed that it was here on the home ground that the real battle would take place. They freely accepted, from the very commencement of the ' Emergency ', that any situation developing from an invasion across the border must, inevitably, be a ' doomsday one '. To that end they were fully resigned to involving as many of their opponents as possible in the ensuing doom.

Great numbers of young men and women had also joined Britain's army, navy and airforce. It is well known that there were more Southern Irish volunteers, per capita, in the British army than there were from the ' loyal ' province of Ulster, or the six annexed counties thereof. These volunteers were predominantly Catholic—some even were I.R.A. Montgomery, or some such big ' brass ', when reviewing troops after the D-day landing, stopped in front of a man who was wearing with his other ribbons one of unusual hues, namely, green, white and orange. ' What's that one then, private ?' he enquired. ' That's me 1916 ribbon ', was the reply. Or so the story goes.

Again, many Irish were working for the good war-time wages in the factories of Britain—glad to get the work too because Ireland, isolated from the outside world and having no resources either of minerals or fuels (other than peat), was unable to keep her own industries fully going. Thanks to de Valera's economic policy of self-sufficiency, there was just enough industry to provide for the nation's basic consumers' needs. All energies were concentrated on agriculture so that it was in this sphere that the country really excelled. Vast quantities of cattle, sheep, poultry, cheese and other high-protein food poured into the British larder, which would have been very bare indeed but for the Irish contribution. All round, Britain was getting the best of the bargain. The price of Ireland's total involvement in this götterdämmerung would have been Britain's relinquishing of her formal claim to suzerainty over Ireland's northern counties.

On the home front there were the civilians; of these, I myself could now be accounted one, having only just been released from school. Illness had brought this about a year earlier than had been intended. I was really no longer sick, but not recovered either. As a semi-invalid or convalescent I signed on at the National College of Art in Dublin and spent the next few years there.

What was the 'Emergency' like from the level of the domestic consumer—and that indeed was what we were—consumers of invaluable scarcities and a damned nuisance undoubtedly? Ireland, as noted, produces neither coal, oil nor natural gas. The tiny amount of petroleum and coal that Britain allowed us to import, on a strict barter arrangement, was just about enough to keep a skeleton bus service, doctors' cars, taxis, and the army going, on a drastically curtailed basis. A doctor could lose his permit to have a car if he were caught taking his children to the seaside. A taxi driver would lose his if he took his fares to even the proximity of a race-course if races were being run. Some cars were propelled by gas which was stored in great dirigibles tethered to the roofs. These and cars or trucks with anthracite gas-burners were permitted to operate as they were not consuming petrol. One may wonder at how their engines ever stood up to this obnoxious gaseous diet. Many vehicles so equipped were suspected of having hidden petrol tanks.

Ninety per cent of urbanites used the humble bike—others a variety of horse-drawn vehicles. To this end a staggering array of wheeled carriages was brought to light. Some were Georgian coaches that had not hit the roads for a century and a half. There were broughams, hansom cabs, landaus, brakes, drays, dog-carts, vans, three-horse omnibuses, hooded phaetons, goat chaises, four-in-hand drags and, of course, the ubiquitous Irish side-car. I remember the side-cars in Eyre Square in Galway during those years and the drivers shouting, 'Two bob a skull to Salthill. A shilling a leg.'

Living as I did near Stillorgan, I depended for my commuting during that time on the old Bray-Harcourt Street railway, now unhappily removed. It possessed a unique mode of transport, the 'Drumm' train. This was an electric train powered by batteries. These batteries were recharged at the terminals every so often. The inventor was an Irishman, Dr Drumm, and as far as I knew, the experiment never went further than the trains built for the Dublin suburban lines. Despite this, these locomotives ran without a hitch for the whole period of the war and many years afterwards. They and some of the lines are gone, but were once our salvation.

Dublin was fortunate too in having a very good electric tram service which had stood the city in good stead during those lean years. It was a somewhat reduced replica of the system Joyce commemorated in *Ulysses*:

> Before Nelson's pillar trams slowed, shunted, changed trolley, started for Blackrock, Kingstown and Dalkey, Clonskea, Rathgar and Terenure, Palmerston park and Upper Rathmines, Sandymount Green, Rathmines, Ringsend and Sandymount Tower, Harold's Cross . . .
> —Come on, Sandymount Green! . . .
> —Start, Palmerston park!

The trams ran, thanks to the limited self-sufficiency that we had in electricity—this in turn was due to the founding fathers having built an enormous hydro-electric dam on the Shannon in the late 'twenties which vastly exceeded, in its capacity to produce electricity, the state's need at the time. Lengthy train journeys in winter were microcosms of the trans-Siberian railway during the revolution. Stories were told of miniature 'Zhivago' type epics being enacted when passengers had to get out in the snow and fell trees.

Dublin relied almost exclusively on gas for cooking purposes. It was severely rationed. Full pressure was only allowed at certain key hours of the day when important meals were being prepared. On the other hand, gas cannot be switched off from the main source like electricity. Millions of cubic feet remained in the pipes. This gave a 'glimmer' in burners but it was strictly forbidden to use it. In spite of this, people did use it. To combat these, the company, wallowing in the inflated title of the Alliance and Dublin Consumers Gas Company, had ' glimmer' men. These men, mounted on bicycles, would descend on unsuspecting householders, walk straight in (for they had legal power of entry) and if they caught you using the ' glimmer' your supply was disconnected forthwith. If you were very fast and switched off before he got to the kitchen, he could still feel around the burners. Any sign of warmth thereabouts was sufficient circumstantial evidence to have one immediately cut off. The alternative, should such draconian steps be taken, would be to cook on an ordinary domestic fire, burning turf. Difficult at the best of times but a real nightmare to the poor Catholic housewife with husband and (inevitably) nine children. For her, it was a disaster too awful to contemplate—and when it did happen the lamentations of grief would put one in mind of an ' American wake'. No wonder the ' glimmer' man was so dreaded. They say now that the car-parking wardens are his direct descendants.

As for food; meat, eggs and milk were in abundant supply though butter and sugar were rationed. That there was sugar at all was again thanks to the founding fathers and their self-reliance programme, which included the growing of sugar beet and the building of factories for the purpose of sugar manufacture. Ireland had always depended on the import of flour for the making of bread as the Irish climate is not suitable for the ripening of wheat. We were now forced to grow it, however imperfectly it ripened. Compulsory tillage was decreed, and every farmer, no matter what size his acreage, had to grow his share of wheat. Even then, to provide the nation's need, the entire ear of wheat had to be used. The result was a very dark brown loaf which was usually somewhat soggy. This was the only fault I could find with it—the fact that it was impossible to bake out its damp content—for otherwise it had a pleasant nutty taste, a property that was greatly enhanced by the application of salty ' farmers' butter ' rather than the purer, bland, and somewhat tasteless 'creamery' butter. There was enough of it to go around.

Clothes and shoes were rationed—but only as a precaution, for there were in fact abundant supplies so that in time one did not even produce coupons. Sweets and cigarettes were very scarce but not rationed. One had to get them by assiduous supplication, guile, blackmail, bribery, or plain begging. Like most boys of my age, I was an addicted smoker, always dying for a smoke. Once at a dance in Ballybunion I turned to a man seated next to me and with all the formality of one about to describe an elaborate gavotte, commenced my supplication with something that ran like this: 'Excuse me, sir, but could you do me a great personal favour . . .' I then asked him plainly to give me a cigarette. He pushed a crumpled Woodbine butt into my beggar's hand and fled mumbling something or other about how there must surely be somewhere in the blankety hall where a body could sit down without a shower of bums descending on him. Oh yes, dignity is an early casualty of war.

There never was any real scarcity of drink. Whiskey could sometimes be in short supply but there was always plenty of Guinness. I only remember one 'drought' as such. I was holidaying in Mitchelstown, county Cork, at a time when large-scale army manoeuvres were taking place in the region. The Southern command was 'at war' with the Eastern command. Like the legions of Xerxes who, in their advance had consumed the Euphrates, they had drunk the province of Munster dry! For about a week while they were in the area, the best you could do for yourself in the way of a jar was a bottle of cider from the nearby works of Bulmer's in Clonmel.

The scarcest, the most-prized commodity of all was tea. The Irish, as we know, are dedicated tea-drinkers. For a half pound of tea they would swap a gammon of ham, a bottle of whiskey or fifty cigarettes, and almost their souls. The more I thought about this phenomenon, the more my wonder grew. Tea, in fact, is neither food nor a drink. It is a vegetable dye. Tomás

Ó Crohan remembered in the middle of the last century cases of tea being washed up on the Great Blasket Island from a clipper that had perished in the Blasket Sound. The islanders, on examination, at length deduced that the stuff was, in fact, a dye, and used it accordingly to colour the petticoats of their womenfolk.

Nevertheless, it is supposed to possess almost supernatural powers of medication by our people generally, but women in particular. The kettle never leaves the hob in Ireland. Its life's work is to provide endless boiling water for the infusion of the miraculous cha-cha herb. Had whiskey or stout disappeared, substitutes could be found (pace Iveagh), and we are adept at home distilling. One could give up cars, and bicycle healthily as a substitute. But there never was a substitute for tea, even in wartime Germany, where they could make ersatz coffee. Once a country gets the taste of it, she is committed in perpetuity to have it doled out to her come hell or high water, even if the stuff has to be transported, as in our case, across half the globe in ancient leaky rust-buckets, through mine and submarine-infested seas.

Looking back on it, there was a lot to be said for the times. There were no cars, but there was no pollution; the variety of food was not great but was at least wholesome. There was nothing, really, in the condition of neutrality that militated against human happiness. The goodness of the simple things was emphasized rather than diminished by the absence of superfluous luxuries. The country was clean, uncluttered and unhurried. There was no tourism. We could not travel abroad nor could the world come to view us. We were less spoiled than now, and the day of the Patrick Pearse Motel and the weekend package trips to Majorca was still wrapped in a delayed-action time-bomb not scheduled to go off for another twenty years.

Tidings of the great struggle did come to us in small manifestations: the mail boats from Holyhead were painted grey and mounted 13-pounder cannon on the fore-decks. Aer

Lingus flew its one-and-only DC-3 Dakota with blacked-out windows to Liverpool. Once in the skies above Dublin I saw a dog-fight between a Messerschmitt and a Spitfire, and some aircraft (Axis and Allied) crash-landed. Leopardstown Racecourse which was hard-by where I lived seemed to be a popular choice as a landing place. And of course we heard of our own cargo vessels bearing the legend EIRE writ large upon their sides together with the tricolour, all illuminated fully by night, being torpedoed and sunk; and mourned the loss of the brave souls that sailed them.

Some bombs did fall at various times and places, and numbers were killed. Dublin had no blackout, only restrictions on display lighting so she must easily have been identifiable as a neutral city. It is unlikely that any of them were dropped deliberately, though some may have been ditched by German bombers evading British night fighters.

There was even a story going the rounds at one time about an American ' Flying Fortress ' lost somewhere over Ireland and that the following conversation took place between the crew on their intercom :

> *Pilot to Navigator* : Where do you figure we now are, Navigator?
> *Navigator to Pilot* : I couldn't rightly say, Sir . . .
> *Pilot to Bombardier* : Okay Bombardier, bawmbs away!

But the chances of a bomb *not* hitting an identifiable slice of Joyce's Dublin would have been indeed small and so sure enough when German bombs did fall, on the night of 31 May 1941, killing many civilians in the North Strand area, they destroyed, inter alia, the premises of H.J. O'Neill, the undertakers who had been in charge of the funeral arrangements for poor Paddy Dignam on Bloomsday.

There were too in Dublin city aggressive little ladies of the Anglo-Irish persuasion who were doing their bit for the Allied war effort by letting out the air in the tyres of the Japanese Ambassador's car. As a further earnest of their belligerence, these diminutive amazons would save their tea and sugar

rations from the F.M. Café or Mitchell's Tea Shop to send to
' the boys in blue '.

At the Chancellery of the German Embassy at 58
Northumberland Road, deft hands frequently re-arranged the
flower pots on the windowsills. After the war we were asked
to believe that the combinations and permutations based on
these arrangements were the apparatus for the code that the
Germans used for communicating with the Irish underground.

Lord Rugby, the British Ambassador, fielded a cricket team
that used to play in Trinity College Park and which included
the former Grattan's ' goalie ', Paddy Kavanagh. The American
Ambassador, (a Mr Grey), was known to call regularly on the
Taoiseach, Mr de Valera, and commit serious, physical violence
on the office furniture because Dev wouldn't play war with
him.

But the best steaks in the world were grilling over the char-
coal at the Dolphin Hotel and there was racing in the Phoenix
Park and white ties and tails at the Shelbourne, while the
whiskey poured niagarously in the Pearl and the Palace bars.
Taking it all in all, it was not the worst ' emergency ' that we,
the Irish, had ever come through.

3

Behind the Emerald Curtain

What seest thou else,
In the dark backward and abysm of time?
Shakespeare: *Richard II*

The Curragh in county Kildare is world renowned as the headquarters of Irish racing. On this immense limestone plateau some of the best racehorses in the world are bred, trained and raced. Here also, the Irish army has its main base. Its strategic setting in the centre of the country is a legacy from the British occupation, when her armies were quick to recognize its tactical advantages.

Even before the fateful Battle of the Boyne, the Curragh was used by the English as a base for nearly 10,000 troops including 5,000 Frenchmen. By 1804, the number quartered there had risen to 13,000, their purpose now being to repel a possible French invasion and, more significantly, ' to show the lower order of the people that troops could be moved to many places in a very short time.' (Desmond Shaw, *Records of the Military History of Ireland*.)

Here for the duration of the Emergency three separate internment camps could be found in close proximity to the military base. The largest housed the IRA, the other two, Allied and Axis prisoners of war. Amongst the many who spent years in the internment camp were Brendan Behan, Tony McInerney, who was later secretary of *Envoy* magazine, Bob Bradshaw and my own brother-in-law, Seán Dunne, who was afterwards Labour member in the Dáil for county Dublin. Despite the confinement, the Irish internees managed to extract something of value during this prolonged period of incarceration by turning the camp into a sort of rough-and-ready

16

B

university in which many skills and languages could be learnt.

In the adjoining camps, small numbers of Luftwaffe personnel, who had strayed or had to 'ditch', were interned according to the Geneva rules concerning belligerent parties found on neutral territory. There were also some German and Italian naval officers and men, as well as merchant seamen. The British camp consisted mainly of members of the RAF who had found cause to 'bale out'. Rumour had it that these were allowed to 'escape' quietly. As the government controlled a tight censorship, it was an official 'non-happening'. The Axis internees had no such hope of return to their countries and had to content themselves with more or less unlimited 'parole'. Sometimes one would see whole parties of them at dress dances in Dublin. At least one of them, who had been a reconnaissance cameraman in the Luftwaffe, stayed on in Ireland after the war, got married to an Irish girl and set up as a very successful photographer!

'Ingrown' would be a fitting description of Irish culture since the birth of the Irish Free State back in 1922. The need to protect this delicate little green plant from the fresh winds of opinion and the germs of new ideas was considered paramount in the order of priorities by the Gaelic mandarins, who behaved as if this was their own private aspidistra. This self-appointed and self-perpetuating oligarchy saw to it that all windows and doors were securely locked and bolted.

The censorship of literature law which the founding fathers, in their sea-green incorruptibility, had managed to have enacted even in the teeth of the brave and eloquent opposition of Senator William Butler Yeats lay like a heavy blight on the cultural landscape of the time. It is still unhappily with us but has greatly curtailed its activities, addressing itself now more to what may be considered overtly pornographic than to that which is manifestly literature. Few writers of any talent escaped its attentions in those days of neutrality, so that in time it became a badge of artistic distinction and intellectual courage to have had at least one book banned.

The establishment was further enabled to indulge its passion with the new ' military ' censorship thanks to the carte blanche which the Emergency Regulations had given them. An example of how grotesque this could be in its application was given in the *Irish Times* just after the Japanese had sunk the aircraft carrier HMS Ark Royal. A pre-war employee had gone down gallantly with the great ship and the paper wished to record and honour the deed, in addition to which the editor (whom we will meet) was staunchly pro-Allied. After a prolonged and frustrating session with the military censor the best he was able to squeeze out of him was permission to print some laconic lines which, if memory serves, went—

' We regret to report that Mr X who formerly worked on the reporting staff of the *Irish Times* has lost his life as the result of a boating incident off Singapore.'

About the same time, a reproduction of Manet's *Olympus* was denounced when Victor Waddington put it on display in his gallery in Anne Street; the Dublin Corporation loftily refused a gift of Rouault's *Christ Crowned with Thorns*; the police had shown sufficient interest in Kavanagh's *The Great Hunger* to pay the author a personal call. Seán O'Faoláin's *Bird Alone* was banned as was Kate O'Brien's *The Land of Spices*. Incredibly Eric Cross's little masterpiece *The Tailor and Ansty* had also received this accolade. Jazz was forbidden to be played on Radio Eireann. In this stifling greenhouse, more hermetically sealed than ever thanks to total war, the sickly, fussed-over verdure wilted, fatally it seemed. That it did not die was no thanks to priest, politician or technocrat, but to poet and painter. It was these, without physical roots, and the dreamers, who finally hurled themselves against that green density of gombeen men, crawling hack, bogus patriot and pietistic profiteer, that found this humidity stimulating in Ireland's green and unpleasant land. Some of them we shall meet in these pages; they were not selected because they were the most outstanding personalities or the most talented, though some demonstrably were in both respects, but because I knew them well and they knew me, and we shared the experience of working together in besieged times when the worst enemy was the one within the gates. They were the keepers of the nation's conscience, these who injected sanity through humour —while partly losing their own in the process.

It was in the streets and pubs of Dublin that I met them in the middle nineteen-forties. Streets which echoed to the ring of hooves and wheels of steel, where along the noiseless wooden sets of Grafton Street brigades of cyclists would at tea-time silently invade the thoroughfare, while distantly the tram bells clanged and the armatures crackled as they crossed the points. Where an aroma of peat smoke hung in the air, where children ran about, even in winter, in bare feet. In a Dublin which was so old and poor, yet for me so young and vital—so unique.

4

Distilled Damnation,
or Bacchus and his Pardners

Be sober, and hope to the end.
St Peter (1 : 13)

Man being reasonable must get drunk;
The best of life is but intoxication.
Byron : *Don Juan*

Most of the Dubliners I knew then had an alcohol problem—
they couldn't get enough of it. The Irish, we are told, are
doughty drinkers—at least by the standards of their end of
Europe, and the Dubliners, it follows, are no better or worse
than the rest.

Much is said, more is sung about the Irishman and his thirst.
Such notables as Brendan Behan and certain Irish film stars,
whose names just now escape me, have given no end of international currency to the myth that we are a fine, carousing
race of hard drinkers, passionately addicted to 'the dhrop'.
On the other hand, Dr Dermot Walsh in the *Journal of
Alcoholism* (Summer 1972) published by the British Medical
Council on Alcoholism, writes 'data from the United States
and the United Kingdom seem fairly consistent . . . that of all
ethnic groups, the Irish are most susceptible to alcoholism.'
However, he goes on to say that the *per capita* consumption
of alcohol in Ireland is low by international standards. He
gives the following figures for the year 1966; Consumption of
alcohol per head of population aged fifteen years and over:
*France: 20.8 litres; West Germany: 11.3 litres; U.S.A.: 7.6
litres; U.K.: 5.9 litres; Republic of Ireland: 5.8 litres.*

Unlike Europe, alcohol is not part of our diet. In civilized
continental countries wine is consumed by the entire family. It

is as much part of the national ration as bread or meat; it should no more be subject to excise than salt. In Ireland, alcohol is not partaken by the family, nor is it served with meals or generally allowed into homes.

Our womenfolk, except for those of the urban population, tend to drink only moderately. Most of the drinking is therefore done by men of mature age. Before distilling a statistic from this lot, we must first subtract the following: priests and religious (of whom we certainly have one of the highest *per capita* ratios in the world), an enormous army of Catholic teetotallers, known as the Pioneer Total Abstinence Association, founded in the last century by Father Theobald Mathew, when hard liquor was what it is not now, cheap and readily available, sober-minded Protestants and Anglo-Irish of steady disposition, lapsed revellers and reformed drunks who have surrendered to wife, church or necessity, God-fearing worshippers of divers persuasions and those who value career and security; the thrifty and the health-conscious and, not to be forgotten, the non-drinkers, of which there are, strange to relate, some resolute few in this Emerald Isle.

The remaining concentrate, or heady residue, amounting to about fifteen per cent of the population, is responsible for the all-over picture of above average nationwide drinking. The true picture is both more comforting and more alarming than we had suspected. It was in the milieu of that fifteen per cent that I shared many of the experiences of this book; for the writers and artists of the forties and fifties were, for better or worse, ardent members of this company. One must be careful not to generalize on this subject. As the man put it, which is more correct: In Dublin the best Irish is drunk? Or, In Dublin the best Irish are drunk?

Cyril Connolly once remarked upon that singular phenomenon whereby no nation—however remote or uncouth—had ever failed to isolate ' alcohol ' from the multitudinous and disparate vegetations of the earth. Ireland was certainly no exception. Her contribution to the world's bacchanalia was nothing less than *whiskey* itself. This is a word which derives from the Gaelic ' uisce beatha ', or water of life. ' The excessive use of whiskey in Dublin,' wrote Sir John Carr, English jurist and tourist in 1803, ' cannot fail to attract the attention of a stranger . . . the number of shops where this liquid poison and other drams are sold is shockingly great.' ' Scotch ' is merely an imitation (and genuine connoisseurs will argue, a bad one!) of the real thing, though it is consumed on a global scale. Where whiskey is still handmade and homemade (without benefit to revenue commissioners or the approval of clergy) in the mountainy fastnesses of Tipperary and Mayo, it is much the same liquor, fermented in the same way, as the Gaels and their predecessors relished so much. It is also said that the Irish, by a further unprecedented stroke of sophistication, ' invented ' soda water, thus making the already palatable drink ambrosial. For reasons unknown, the idea of blending the two did not occur to anyone until some considerable time after the actual invention. Bryon urges, ' Wine and women, mirth and laughter—sermons and soda-water the day after!' suggesting that it was considered more a remedy than an adjunct, even thirty years after its introduction.

The Irish allow that the ' creature ' has great curative powers *in extremis;* as distinct from tea which is continuously health-giving. The old lag with lumbago in Behan's *The Quare Fella* assures us that there are medicinal virtues in the consumption of even the more extreme forms of the spirit as he quaffs the bottle of methyl alcohol which has been prescribed purely as a lubricant, in his case, for muscular massage, observing thought-fully after what would be for most a death-dealing dose of C_2H_2 OH: ' There's a cure in that against the cold and the want of the world. . . .' Later we shall meet the ' Gingerman ' with his happy, precocious and anticipatory cries of ' The meths, the meths . . .!'

Patrick Kavanagh had dreams of making the stuff himself. Boyhood memories of ' the remote places of Donaghmoyne where the poteen was made ' must have prodded him. One day

he brought up the subject with me and, to my amazement—
quite seriously. He knew the ingredients required for moon-
shine and the whole distillation process. What was holding
him up was the expertise required in the making of the
' worm '—that spiral copper tube down which the evaporated
wash condenses to give the spirit. He thought that asking for
one at an ironmongery or requesting a plumber to make one
up might excite suspicion. I was able to tell him an old trick
we had when shaping exhaust pipes for motor bikes or boats :
get your eight-foot length of ordinary two inch copper pipe.
Fill it with sand and pack each end with a wooden stop. Using
a tin drum or even a bucket as a ' jig ', put a blow-lamp to the
tubing and slowly shape the pipe around the drum as required.
The sand will prevent kinking or cracking at the bends. Afterwards unplug and let the sand out. Instant wor-um!

Infinitely bendable plastic pipes—like colour television and
de-hydrated potato mash—were still encapsulated within the
womb of time; undreamt of too was the niagara of Scotch
which would await his pleasure in the years to come—pipes,
plastic or copper notwithstanding.

My own mother told me how during the great 'flu epidemic
of 1918-1919 the district nurse in her part of south Tipperary
travelled from house to house in her pony and trap with a
large milk churn of poteen which she dispensed liberally to
the young and old of both sexes, and how it was an unqualified
success, nay, an incomparable specific, infallible cure and
sovereign remedy for this terrifying ailment. Some believed
that the actual influenza virus got so drunk from the hard
stuff, in its journey down the victim's gullet, as to be rendered
incapable of fulfilling its lethal functions.

Alas for the poteen, it is illegal and becoming harder to get,
particularly the ' good stuff ' reputed to be kept for the priest
or, better again, the station sergeant. We law-abiding citizens
must make do with the official product or authorized version
of the liquor upon which duty has been paid—that is to say,
Irish. This is a whiskey which deserves to be much better

known abroad, far excelling Scotch in the opinion of many connoisseurs. If it has a fault, then it is that it is too good—in which case the world does not deserve it.

ɪﻛﻌﻴﻘﺌﻜﻤﺌ

The Bona is blazing to-night and the black tar is melting away
And the melodeon breathes the war-dance of this St John's Eve.
I would go back . . .

Those lines, from *Evergreena* by Patrick Galvin, may have nothing to do with what I am about to discuss, but for some reason they haunt me.

In the early 'forties, a system legalizing the hours of drinking existed (in other words, that made drinking an unlawful occupation except at hours and in places decreed by bureaucrats and petty officials) that had been handed down by the previous landlords, the British. The Act which principally governed the consumption of beer, wine and spirits was summed up in the one word DORA. This was not the code name of a hurricane, but the initials of The Defence of the Realm Act, and was part of Lloyd George's legacy to the holy country of Ireland. Another of the Welsh Wizard's gifts was the Black and Tans.

His Act, introduced during the first world war, was designed to take the British munitions worker off the bottle—and into battle. Perhaps he had read Dryden or, at least, some lines from *Cymon and Iphigenia,*

Of seeming arms to make a short essay,
Then hasten to be drunk, the business of the day.

The stop-go system of permitted drinking hours peculiar to these off-shore islands, so cherished by florid Tory magistrates and whey-faced Irish lay apostles alike, are the bane of the honest drinking man and the wonder of the rest of the world.

In the time that we are remembering, that side-show of the DORA charade, the full *bona fide* law was open for business. I say 'full' because many readers will be thinking of the attenuated *bona fide* regulations which they experienced. Briefly, a *bona fide* traveller was one who *bona fide* (in good faith) was honestly journeying (by horse or foot) and, for the purposes of survival required refreshment, both liquid and solid—with a strong preference for the latter. Licensed houses (pubs) were obliged to provide such victuals at any time during the day or night. There was, in addition, the provision that water and fodder should be provided for the man's horse which, for all I know, may yet be on the statute book.

In those arcadian days, it was possible, legally, to drink all night, providing one had accomplished the business of covering the three miles that was the statutory 'journey' establishing your claim as a traveller. Of course, with the war on and the absence of cars or any mechanized transport for that matter, travellers were few and such that existed probably were genuinely *bona fide*, God help them. I once experienced the sensation of being fully *bona fide*. A few of us set out on bicycles and, having pedalled the all-important three miles, sought, and nearly obtained, comfort under the old Act. This necessitated the knocking-up of Matt Smith of Stepaside (a hamlet sleeping on the Dublin foothills) in the wee hours. It was a frosty night; an upstairs window was flung open and an irate landlord's head emerged.

'What do yeez want?'
'Weez is bonafeeds.'
'Let yez get the hell outa here or I'll call the guards.'
'We can't. Weez is travellers. Really, weez is.'
'Yeez will not hop that ball here.'
'Looka, ya don't think weez'd be botherin' ya at this houra the mornin' unless weez was really bonafeeds?'
'Yeez have yez'r galue. Where are yeez supposed to be travellin'?'
'Ballybunion.'

' Where have yeez come from? '

' Ballybock.'

' Jeezus! '

After much ado, we were eventually allowed in. He let us have a pint in the darkened snug, but nagged us so much (' Are yeez near finished yet?') that the drink turned flat and we soon departed. It was my only experience of drinking legally after hours.

Later in the 'forties, this law was amended. Under the new dispensation, the *bona fide* traveller could drink for one hour only after the legal closing time (usually 10.30 pm) of the city pubs, instead of all night as before. But whereas the old code was rarely exploited except, perhaps, on the odd occasion when the publican was entertaining friends, or when the press of business in the bars was sufficient to warrant the losing of several hours of his sleep, the new one was an instant success (no doubt, beyond anything the parliamentary draughtsman had envisaged) and for a decade or so it became a great Irish social phenomenon and cod.

The motor cars were back so that the ' three mile ' journey was within the competence of anyone who could thumb a lift. The publicans (they had to be outside the city boundaries) welcomed this new development all the more so, since it concentrated more business into one hour than they would normally have expected to do in a weekend. For the public it was all a lark. As soon as the town pubs closed the night people took to their cars and struck out for the mountainy bonafeeds where a merry hour or so was put in by all. There was about it that carnival, Australian atmosphere that so often attends the accomplishment of a deed standing somewhat up to weather of the law.

There would be periodic checks to test the authenticity of our *bona fides*. When the guards would raid the pubs and quiz us as to our origins, the atmosphere would become electric with subterfuge and intrigue. Invariably, the majority would be locals living within the precious three miles, unable to drag themselves away from the ' scene of the action '. Most people learnt to lie fluently and were equally adept at producing documentary proof to back up the lies.

Why the law was brought to pass in the first instance, and what principle it was designed to promote, we are not to enquire. It seemed to have neither a pragmatical objective nor an ethical goal. If its purpose was to enforce sobriety, it encouraged drunkenness. If the aim was to tighten up the old Act, the target it achieved was that of liberating and bringing its advantage to a broader public. It may have been the most absurd, the most ludicrous, of all the amending Acts that our native bureaucracy has, with unwearying application, fabricated for this nation in the first fifty years of its political existence—though I doubt it. Anybody with even a nodding acquaintanceship of that great national attic of accumulated bumpf, the Acts of Parliament, would be reluctant to single out any one document as worthy of the distinction of being the *most* ridiculous.

The only tangible evidence now of the old *bona fides* is the nimbus of gaudy roadhouses that straddle the main roads radiating from Dublin. These had once been the humble inns of hamlet and village which, bloated from the *bona fide* boom, doubled in size and burst out into neon lighting, foam-rubber seating, wall-to-wall carpeting, Musak and the other appurtenances of the Great Society. That's why the outer suburbs of Dublin sometimes remind visiting Americans of a poor man's Las Vegas.

᛫ᚾᛖᛝᛁᚳᚻᛁ᛫

The Palace and the Pearl bars were the haunts of the established and the aspiring literati, and the burrows of poetaster and journalist in those days. You didn't have to go far to find the reason. They were the nearest oases to the *Irish Times*, a paper which, even then, had pretensions to a cultural identity, supposedly not shared by the other two dailies—the *Irish Press* and the *Irish Independent*.

Bertie Smyllie, the editor, was a man of Chestertonian proportions, who presided over the ' salon ' in the back room (' lounge ' would be too much) of the Palace, the more ' arty ' of the two taverns. If Smyllie (wedged in his chair, looking like a stranded bull walrus, a large ball of malt in his chubby hand) even nodded at you—you had it nearly made.

* The paper had the power to put money in the pocket of poet and writer—and money in those austere days was as rare as hen's teeth. P-p-p-patrick C-c-campbell, as well as Myles na gCopaleen, wrote daily columns for him then, and I remember T.H. White once giving it as his opinion that Campbell was the better of the two. Tony Gray was also with the paper then as well as several lesser talents who later made a name for themselves, so Smyllie had some justification in seeing himself as the Lorenzo the Magnificent of Westmoreland Street.

Heavier or more sustained drinking than took place in Pearl and Palace during those years may never have occurred before or will again—it is still remembered with awe by the old timers. It might have had something to do with the war, for there was little to spend money on and, as I have said, drink itself was not scarce. Chat never is in Dublin, and we must only imagine what novels and poems and plays drifted up and lodged with the nicotine in the ceilings of those hostelries.

Rumours of literary goings-on in MacDaid's must have reached the master's ear because Smyllie turned up there one night, having made the prodigious journey (of about half a mile) from the Palace. It was about the time that this pub was beginning its long history as a poetic glue-pot. A fight over the use of spondees was going on in one corner between two wild men in duffle coats, Brendan Behan was standing on a table bawling his rendition of ' I was Lady Chatterly's Lover ' and Gainor Crist, the Ginger Man, was getting sick, evidently into someone else's pint. It was too much for the great man, who finished, in one vast swallow, his large Irish, gave a final, baleful owl-like glare at this frightening assembly, and waddled out into the Harry Street night and the ultimate sanctuary of the Palace as fast as his trotters could take him. He was never seen in McDaid's again.

The Bailey came sometime later—in 1956. It was, in fact, more a restaurant in its pre-Ryan incarnation, although it had a small cocktail bar. They never really wanted the literati to use it either, for they barred Paddy Kavanagh for wearing his hat on the premises—a hard fate for him then as he probably even slept in it! The Bailey played an insignificant role in the first years of the period under examination, but had played quite a considerable part in the artistic and political life in Dublin during the preceding hundred years. Notably, it was the favourite haunt of Arthur Griffith, founder of Sinn Féin, editor of the *United Irishman*, and later President of Dáil Eireann. Others who frequented it regularly were James Stephens, Oliver St John Gogarty, AE (George Russell) and even James Joyce himself.

When I took over as licensee, I set about restoring the original atmosphere as much as possible, and it again became a meeting-place for actors, painters and writers. The building was very old.

In the middle-sixties a city tenement had collapsed, killing six people. The Dublin Corporation panicked and started demolishing buildings right, left and centre. The old Bailey caught its all-seeing eye. One day a man in dun-coloured gaberdine and a pork-pie hat called on me. He was from the Dangerous Building Section. I took him on a guided tour of the premises. I had taken great care to see that all was spotless and that most cracks and fissures were adequately filled in.

As we toured, I continuously pressed home the point that, though the premises was antique, it had stood up splendidly to the ravages of time; that, as venerable buildings went, it was in good heart; in a word—the premises was in sound ' nick '.

He answered with never a word but his features under the

rim of the pork-pie hat shrunk inwards like a tiny clenched fist.

The tour finished, he signalled that we should cross to the other side of the street. We stood there in silence for about two minutes. A fine curtain of grey rain was by now encompassing us. Slowly he raised a gaberdined arm and aimed it generally in the direction of the Bailey. His head tilted back and a rain drop fell from his nose. I knew that he was about to speak; that a pronouncement was now imminent.

' All that will have to come down ', he cried.
' But, but . . . ', I protested.
' Sure the joyces is walking out of it! ' he further exclaimed.

And that was the end of life in the ' old ' Bailey. The Joyces and all the others had indeed finally walked out of it.

By the next post I received a thirty-day demolition order. In time, a new Bailey sprang from the ruins of the old, but it could not be much more than what I made it, a reasonably decent modern pub—neither Ye Olde nor Colour Supplement Pseudo, but it has little relevance to this narrative—except that it continued to be a Dublin ' centre ' much used by all the original McDaidian characters, and became exclusively Paddy Kavanagh's pub in the last year of his life.

' The pubs ', says Joyce Cary in *The Horse's Mouth*, ' know a lot; almost as much as the churches. They've got a tradition.' which reminds me that there is one pub in Dublin that became a church and one church that became a pub! McDaid's (of all places) used to be a Moravian Church (trust it) while the Church of the Blessed Sacrament in D'Olier Street used to be The Red Bank, pub-come-fish-bar. When the latter re-opened as an ecclesiastical establishment, the *Evening Press* ran a pietistic headline bearing the legend:

' ALL DUBLIN ON ITS KNEES '

When Benedict Kiely read this in Flynn's adjacent premises, he was heard to remark, ' that should read:

"SOUL ON THE BONE"

If they ever build our long-threatened folk museum, they must at least give us a replica of a genuine Irish country pub—perhaps (come to think of it) a working model. It will have low rafters and the whitewash on the ceiling will be much discoloured by turf smoke from an open hearth. The floor will have large irregular flags. The counter will be low—so that you would have to sit on a barrel to rest your arms on it. There will be forms around the walls and an oil lamp hanging from a beam. There will be a clock with a large yellowing face. It will annunciate the passing of time in modulated tones. It will have a calming influence because its tick will just be that much slower than your own heartbeat. By way of ornament, on the wall will hang a richly cut glass mirror, which will also proclaim the virtues of some long-vanished brand of whiskey. There will be many good things sold as well as beer, wines and spirits; like roofs for clay pipes, hob-nailed boots, pitchfork handles, Indian meal, storm lanterns, dried ling and packets of Mrs Cullen's Powders. And the stout will be served from a combination of jugs and basins in a ritual as exacting as the Japanese tea ceremony. Somebody seated near the fire may scrape an old fiddle. And there will be no colour television or musak, and folk will talk quietly.

But it's a ball of malt to a small soda-water they never will.

5

Overtures and Beginners

On the stage he was natural, simple, affecting,
'Twas only that, when he was off, he was acting.
(Oliver Goldsmith on Garrick)

I had trod the boards by this time (though Hecuba might well have wondered what she had done to deserve me), and despite the fact that my subsequent and more serious entrance to theatre was through the door of the scene dock, I was a veteran spear-holder before I was twenty years old.

I had played leads in school plays so that when I heard that the company of Sheila Richards and Michael Walsh needed a 'walk-on', I was not at all modest about applying for the job. The salary was ten shillings a week. I appeared in several productions in which, as I say, I held spears and conveyed in a general fashion the significant message that the carriage awaited without. But the production that stands out in high relief on the tablets of my memory is Shaw's *Saint Joan*. Wilfred Bramble (later to become famous as the elderly 'junky' in the television series 'Steptoe and Son' played the part of the demented, conscience-stricken English friar outstandingly well. Other parts, almost as small as my own were played by Daniel O'Herlihy (later to become a film star and a nominee for an Oscar) and Edward Mulhare, who took over from Rex Harrison in the Broadway production of *My Fair Lady*, Aidan Grennell and many others.

I played one of the brutal and licentious soldiery whose task it was to stand guard over the prisoner, Joan of Arc, during the long trial scene. Now we were playing during the month of August and it was a particularly hot one that year. Johnny Hughes and I were clad in chain-mail, also helmets and visors, in which drag we had to stand to attention while Shaw's arguments wandered about the stage in their usual leisurely fashion.

The chain-mail catsuits were a legacy from Laurence Olivier's filming of Henry V in Wicklow the previous year (1944) and were not, in fact, chain-mail at all. They were made of very heavy natural Aran wool, knitted and painted black and silver to simulate the real thing. Standing in this garb and holding a spear, one felt like Amundsen implanting his flag on the South Pole—for indeed in this costume one was correctly togged out for the Antarctic.

Johnny and I stood on a rostrum up-stage. As mere objects or scenery we must have cut quite a dramatic figure, as a whole battery of huge spots had been brought to bear on us—adding immeasurably to the already unbearable heat.

Came a Saturday matinee in the middle of the heatwave. I was doing my thing on the rostrum. Rolling periods of Shavian dialogue wafted about me. I felt as though I had been lowered into an incinerator. The next thing I knew was that I was lying back-stage and that someone was putting a glass of brandy to my lips. I remembered Groucho Marx in a film in like circumstances, with closed eyes, hissing, ' *force brandy through my teeth!* '

It seems my timing had been perfect. At the very moment in the play, the climactic one when Joan, at bay, turns on her persecutors, who have now promised merely perpetual solitary confinement instead of death at the stake in exchange for her recanting everything she holds true, faces the inquisition and flings, like hot coals, in its face, that line :

' I say to you therefore that your council is not of God but of the devil! '

At this moment, as the bishops and abbots rent their garments, with cries of ' Blasphemy! ' and ' Burn! Burn! ' I keeled over like an axed elm and crashed unconscious into the wings. It was such an appropriate—such a wholly sympathetic—response that few of the audience realized that anything had gone amiss.

D

Like the good storm trooper that I was, I turned up for the evening performance. But what an exit it had been— what a way to go!

⟨✦⟩

Anew MacMaster and Micheál MacLiammóir towered above the theatrical world of the day. It was the golden age of the Gate where the Edwards-MacLiammóir-company shared the lease of the building with the Earl of Longford's deservedly popular repertory company.

The isolation brought about by war had made us look to ourselves for distraction and entertainment. With the scramble for worldly prizes temporarily shelved, cultural awareness grew; these were contemplative times, in which people read more books, listened to more concerts, patronized more theatres. Magazines were launched, film societies founded—even our symphony orchestra was born. Above all, the theatre flourished; for the winds that the war blew were not all ill.

The first play I ever saw at the Gate—and this at the very outset of the wa . . . (excuse me) the Emergency, was the Edwards-MacLiammóir production of Shakespeare's *Julius Caesar* in modern dress. To young unjaded eyes it was a stunning *tour-de-force*. All the culture and sophistication of the world was there. And how incredibly up to date it was . . . how refreshingly modern!

Edward Gordon Craig, the father of modern theatre design, had worked for the early Abbey at the beginning of the century, while Tanya Moisewitch had worked for it during the 'thirties. But Hilton Edwards had introduced imaginative and functional lighting for the first time. Used in the action of the performers as well as the flow and texture of the drama, a play was now, for the first time, an exciting visual experience —as well as a hoped-for intellectual reward.

Later I was to work as a set designer myself and to design more than forty productions. My first introduction to this world came from Sean Kenny, the most original theatrical designer of our times. He was an old friend of mine; we had in common Tipperary parents, and I had been best man at his wedding.

A new theatre was opened in the 'fifties—the Eblana. It was part of a bus terminal and had originally been designed as a news-cinema. As events turned out, this plan had never come to pass, and it had lain, subterranean and fallow, for many years, until a young impresario, Eamonn O'Higgins, persuaded the transport ministry to lease it to him as a theatre.

The first production was to be Synge's *Deirdre of the Sorrows*. Anthony Page was to direct and Sean Kenny to design it. Sean asked me to help him with the work and that was how I got my start. Designed as a cinema, the Eblana had no stage. Providing this was our first priority. To make matters worse, there were neither wings nor flies or, for that matter, scene-dock or paint-loft. In fact, there was no access to the stage except through the auditorium.

We had to paint most of the scenery out on the streets (whenever a traffic lull permitted), take it to pieces, bring it back into the theatre and re-assemble it. It was as rough and ready an introduction to the business as one could ask for— designed either to kill or cure. Nothing in the theatre ever seemed impossible after that. But this was all in the future.

Anew MacMaster is commemorated in a splendid portrait by Genaro in the National Gallery. He is depicted wearing the costume he wore in *Othello*. There are few towns in the four provinces of Ireland that had not seen ' Mac ' in these sumptuous Moorish robes. The usual parochial hall or cinema where they played on tour did not run to the luxury of dressing-rooms or wardrobes, so it was Mac's habit to set out on foot for the ' theatre ' in the full splendour of his costume and make-up, regardless of weather.

Carefully choosing the middle of the street and fastidiously lifting his skirts to every puddle, he would make a stately progress, followed by amazed small boys (who might have thought he was at least a cardinal) as he imparted manual, beringed benedictions, through a corridor of gaping rustics. ' The play, dears . . . opening at nine of the clock. Othello, dears . . .' he would inform the bystanders as he passed by with immense strides. He saw no point in losing a good opportunity for plugging business.

He stood a good six foot three—which was right and proper for the last of the great actor-managers. Pat Leatham who once played Desdemona on tour to this most exotic of Othellos, has good reason to recall the performance. They were playing Scarriff at the time, a soporific kraal on the shores of Lough Derg, and the birthplace of the novelist, Edna O'Brien.

For the stupendous strangling scene, Mac always stripped to the waist. The justification for this was that the Moor was going to bed anyhow. But the real purpose was to exhibit the magnificent MacMaster torso (liberally coated with lots of Number Four—dear).

On this particular night, and for no particular reason, Mac had risen to unprecedented histrionic heights. Pat, a young American girl on her first tour, and to whom all this was new, was quite overwhelmed by the occasion. The half-naked torso, towering and glistening above her, the periods of sublime poetry spoken with such nobility, such superb panache, the hushed hall. . . Before she could stop herself she was sobbing uncontrollably . . .

Mac, the old pro, was quick to grasp the danger of the situation. He acted decisively to lower the emotional temperature. Switching his role immediately to melodramatic villain and putting on his most exaggerated cockney accent, he ad-libbed a whispered encouragement which could be heard in the front row: ' Down't let it git yah down, dearee . . .' After that, her problem was how to stop laughing.

I remember another occasion when Mac was playing *Hamlet* in Ballyporeen, a drowsy community nestling in the lower undulations of the Galtee mountains. The lighting arrangements in the village hall were something less than perfect.

Eventually, it exasperated Mac to the extent that in the middle of the crucial ' dagger ' speech, he felt compelled to do something drastic about it. As he got to the lines: ' For who would bear the whips and scorns of time, the oppressor's wrong . . .' (he stepped nimbly into the wings. Noises off suggested the re-positioning of a ' perch ' spot and the replacement of a ' gel ') *Creekk*! . . . ' the proud man's contumely . . .' AWKKK! . . . ' the pangs of despis'd love, the law's delay . . .' (now he calmly emerged, taking his stance once more addressing himself to the bare bodkin) . . . ' the insolence of office, the spurns that patient merit of the unworthy takes, when he himself might his quietus make with a bare bodkin?'

' That's better, dears ', I heard him whisper to himself, as he noticed, with satisfaction, that the lime which had before thrown a distracting white beam at his feet, was now suffusing his distinguished features with a becoming rose-tinted glow. For those who would learn more of this immortal thespian, there are the books of his brother-in-law, Micheál MacLiammóir and a hard-to-get essay in book form called *Mac* by Harold Pinter, who spent a season touring with the great man. He summed him up thus: ' He was a realist. But he possessed a true liberality of spirit. He was humble. He was a devout anti-puritan. He was a very great piss-taker.'

In those days, Alan Simpson was a young officer in the Irish army and a friend of our family, who somehow managed to combine his neo-belligerent activities with being stage-manager (not that they are so dissimilar) for the Edwards-MacLiammóir company. Later, he achieved fame when he and Carolyn Swift founded the Pike Theatre, giving the public, among other things, the first performance of Brendan Behan's *The Quare Fella*. Sometimes he would call meetings at the barracks when he was duty officer and could not get time off. He would be in full uniform, carrying a loaded service revolver, as we sat around a table discussing costumes and props; this military ' presence ' maybe explains why we almost invariably agreed with him on these occasions.

Hilton Edwards was a tireless perfectionist—his lighting re-
hearsals could, and frequently did, go on throughout the
night and Alan, being the stage manager, was always directly
in the line of fire. I had great sympathy for him.

Later, he and I produced *The Scatterin'*, a musical play by
James McKenna which was to be a theatrical landmark in
Dublin, and, arguably, the world's first Rock musical. As a
result, we were invited to put it on in Joan Littlewood's theatre
workshop in Stratford East. We collaborated in many other
productions too, notably, *Waiting for Godot*, *Fursey*—based on
Mervyn Wall's novel—and Dominic Behan's not easily to be
forgotten *Posterity Be Damned* which we put on in the old
Metropolitan music hall in the Edgware Road in London—a
production which very nearly brought the house down—more
so since an extreme republican faction, disliking the play's
theme, had promised to dynamite the building!

The Abbey I knew well enough at that time. My sister
Kathleen had studied at the Abbey School of Acting. I well
remember her and Dan O'Herlihy in a production of Thomas
Dekker's *A Shoemaker's Holiday* at the Peacock, which was
the Abbey's experimental theatre, early in the war. I saw
many of the Abbey favourites in those years, notably the
O'Casey classics: *The Plough and the Stars*, *The Shadow of
a Gunman* and *Juno and the Paycock*. Kathleen went into
films after the war, starring in several movies including Carol
Reed's *Odd Man Out*. This was a film with an Irish setting
(Belfast and the IRA—prophetically enough) which was made
in 1948. Many of the surviving pioneers of the Abbey, whose
contribution to world theatre had been their unique style of
realistic acting, appeared in that film, including F.J.
McCormick, who shared with Barry FitzGerald the distinction of being the greatest actor the Abbey ever produced.

Odd Man Out was made at Pinewood Studios. By one of
those strange coincidences which history so regularly and
impishly provides, ' Pinewood ' was the country mansion in
which the treaty setting up the Irish Free State was negotiated
in 1921 between Lloyd-George and Churchill on the one

hand and Michael Collins and Arthur Griffith on the other. The bar of the canteen was the actual room in which the document had been signed.

The Stormont authorities of the day refused J. Arthur Rank permission to make the film in Belfast; they felt that the film's sympathy lay (however lightly) with the Republican resistance. As a result the streets of Belfast had to be meticulously re-created in Pinewood.

Being in London at the time, I made several visits to the set to see the making of this film; it was a memorable experience from many angles. Robert Newton, for instance, playing the whiskey-artist (said to have been modelled on Sean O'Sullivan) laying about him with relish in the scene where he demolishes a bar with his walking stick. This scene had to be set up several times—not at the instigation of Carol Reed but on Newton's own insistence. He obviously enjoyed beating up a pub—however vicariously. When he came to Ireland for a holiday sometime afterwards, he stayed with us, and I remember having the dread that he would pull the same stunt in the bar of Jammet's! Attired in stained tropical ' ducks ' and armed with a malacca cane, he seemed eager to repeat the performance in a genuine atmosphere. I had to (gently but firmly) ease him out of the place.

But best of all was to watch ' F. J. ' giving the performance of his life. It was, in fact, the last performance of his life, and posterity is fortunate in having this faithful record of an incomparable actor. It is thought that the conditions under which McCormick had to work during *Odd Man Out,* notably days of filming under conditions of simulated rain and sleet, brought about his death shortly after the film's completion.

In the main, it was a low period in the Abbey. Most of the work done was Abbey *manque*—beside which even parody pales. Such is the destiny of great creative enterprises when they fall into the hands of tasteless men. For against enthroned vulgarity, talent, energy and resourcefulness—all labour in vain.

I had the distinction of playing the lead in the last play

Lennox Robinson directed. He was the author of many plays, most notably, *The Far-Off Hills* and *Crabbed Youth and Age,* and had been manager of the Abbey Theatre from 1910 to 1923 when he became a director. The play was called *The Morning of the Wedding.* It was some sort of Czechoslovakian one-act farce in which I played the bridegroom who wakes up in bed on the crucial morn with the wrong woman. It was performed in the Arts Club in Fitzwilliam Street. Lennox must have thought highly of the play—though it caused me acute embarrassment—but whose *chef-d'oeuvre* it was utterly escapes me.

He was at the time, and for some years before his death (1958) Chairman of this same United Arts Club of which I also was a member. The Club, then a glorified after-hours pub, had about as much to do with art as the *News of the World* has to do with literature. Amongst its considerable accomplishments was to have ' black-balled ' the poet Patrick Kavanagh. It was generally known around town as the United Arthritis Club.

Lennox was in the chair at a memorable Annual General Meeting which was, in some ways, as good as anything he ever wrote. He was by now ' Dr ' Robinson, having picked up one of those University doctorates which are dispensed here in lieu of titles. He was looking more pre-Raphaelite than usual, entwined about a chair like a ' snake ' illustration from the Book of Kells. The club's secretary was reading out and proposing in turn the various items on the agenda as they came up. The chairman wilted visibly under the boredom of it all— the very picture of poetic torpor. Presently the secretary, having read the minutes of the preceding AGM, came to the item of the re-election of the club's auditors—a purely automatic annual procedure. The following exchange ensued:

Hon. Sec. :   Item 4. Re-election of our accountants, Messrs.
               Kennedy and Crowley.
Chairman :   Really, I don't see why we should have to be
               pestered by people wishing to become members.

After all, it is the Annual General Meeting . . . I mean to say . . . All this should be handled at ordinary committee level . . .

Hon. Sec.: But, Doctor, they're not just ordinary members . . .

Chairman: Frankly, I couldn't care less who they are or how extraordinary they are—though obviously they mean a lot to *you,* but as far as I'm concerned . . .

(*Voice from the back of the hall*):

Speak up, Dr Robinson. We can't hear a word you're saying.

Chairman: Of course you can't, Molly—you're stone deaf! Let's get on with the next business! I'll not hear Kelly and Crawford's application now—that's certain.

(*Secretary, much agitated, whispers something urgently into the chairman's ear. Slowly the light of understanding begins to dawn on the Gothic features.*)

Chairman: (Rising) So sorry . . . Messrs. McAuley and Clarke . . . Oh, I am *so* sorry . . . The people who do our books. Yes, bless them. The people who do our books.

(CURTAIN)

6

Liffeysiders

Dublin was a town of 'characters' then as now, and I suppose will ever be. A man I knew was taking a stroll down Grafton Street one day when he happened to overhear part of a discussion which three citizens were having outside Mitchell's cafe. The gist of their dialogue was that they were deploring the absence from the Dublin scene of any *real* 'characters'. They appeared to be genuinely aggrieved. They were, in fact, Myles na gCopaleen, Sean O'Sullivan and Brendan Behan. Here you have the essence of the Dublin 'character'; complete unawareness of the fact that he is one himself. Is Dublin particularly prone to this species or is it that we seem to cherish it and therefore record it lovingly? From Buck Mulligan to Blazes Boylan, and Molly Bloom to the Citizen, Joyce's Dublin was as full of characters as the Great Saltee Island is full of gannets: not the least of these were himself and his father.

One heard a lot of the legendary Endymion then, though the 'Bird' Flanagan was considered to have been the patron saint of Dublin characters. Endymion it was however, who, having purchased a ham at an 'Italian warehouse' chose to leave it hanging on its line, then much later returned and, acting with the maximum amount of suspiciousness, 'stole' it from under the eyes of the alerted police, whom he then led on a merry chase through the streets that culminated in his arrest and subsequent embarrassed acquittal. One story of 'Bird' Flanagan was that he was leaving a banquet in Iveagh House in an open carriage. At the last moment he remembered that he had left his gloves behind. He apologized to his lady and asked her to wait. In a matter of moments he returned—by air. He had gone upstairs, opened a window and, with a mighty leap, hurled himself at the cab, landing noisily, but quite neatly, precisely beside his companion. In fairness to the eighteenth-century character ' Buck ' Whaley, it must be said that a similar caper is attributed to him a full century earlier.

I knew one who marvellously mispronounced words—completely unconsciously. He talked about a steep, narrow and dangerous street being a ' vertical ' death trap, and of looking for somebody in every ' conceitable ' place. He sold miscellaneous scrap and bric-à-brac which he referred to as ' antiquarians '. A real Dublin ' character '. Jimmy O'Dea was an even greater character than his creation Biddy Mulligan, ' The Pride of the Coombe ', while Stephen Behan, father of Brendan, was the most delightful of them all. You don't have to be from Dublin to be a Dublin character, as we shall shortly know by our observations of O'Mahony and Myles na gCopaleen—but living there probably increases your chances. Alan C. Breeze got a half page in the *Sunday Times* on the occasion of his bringing T. S. Eliot's false teeth back to Ireland. He needed no character references! Another one I knew went around Dublin for days in clanking chain-mail because, when he returned from a fancy dress ball he had been attending, he found that his *only* real suit had been stolen.

But there were so many of them; Lennox Robinson looking like the spine of an Aubrey Beardsley book with his miniature poodle and the twenty-foot lead attached thereto; the perennial Mayor ' Alfie ' Byrne of the immaculate cut-away coat and waxed moustache; the Envoy Extraordinary and Minister Plenipotentiary of the Dalcassian Kingdom in his Embassy in Charlemont Street; Andy McGee, the Toucher Byrne, and the man who wrote Love, Joy and Peace everywhere.

The daddy of them all had been Jonathan Swift himself, and that is why the true Dubliner has a special place in his heart for the Great Dean. In his will he decreed that the special silver casket in which the document conferring on him the freedom of the City of Cork, be left to his friend the tailor, Paddy McGirk, for use as a container for the special brand of plug tobacco that he chewed. Now he was what you might call a Dublin character.

Young as I was, I was on chatting or nodding acquaintance with many of the prominent public characters and oddities of that wartime scene down there by the Liffeyside—Dublin being the largest village in the world.

A friend, Lionel Miskin, the English painter and writer, often spent holidays with our family. He had once been arrested for doing a painting of the lock of the Grand Canal at Portobello Bridge. Under our relentless Emergency regulations, such innocent artefacts were labelled ' top secret '. The lock, as picturesque as a Constable weir, was a hundred and fifty years old at the time, and served the purpose of elevating or lowering the barges that consigned our quotient of turf (to keep the home fires burning) from furthest Edenderry during these tumultuous years.

On his instigation we made so bold as to visit Jack B. Yeats in his studio in Fitzwilliam Square. He received us kindly, even to the extent of offering us a glass of madeira. I became a good friend, and frequent visitor on Thursday afternoons, which he kept free for random callers.

He kept in a bureau in his studio hundreds of small sketch books (each about the size of a pocket diary) in which were stored the visual ' notes ' which were the source and inspiration of the splendid glowing canvases of his final years. I spent many hours rummaging amongst these books. There was often a gap of as much as forty years between the sketch and the painting. One day Yeats, glancing through a sketch book, would pause at a page; the vision of a half century earlier would return—and, on an ecstatic impulse, he would celebrate the return by committing the memory with characteristic bravura to canvas.

He painted *sub rosa*. There was always a rosebud attached to the highest point of his easel. It served some mystical purpose—although I never thought to ask. His benign figure, stooped with age, radiated gentleness, while his painterly eyes darted hither and thither in quest of images—as though there was time yet for another thousand pictures. He was the most truly great and good man I had ever known.

Margaret Burke Sheridan, the famous soprano, was a delightful ornament of the scene. Brought up as an orphan by the Dominican nuns in the west of Ireland (who were intelligent enough to know that she had a unique gift for singing) she was, thanks to their encouragement, able to study music and singing in Dublin. In time she became a professional, joining the La Scala Opera while yet scarcely more than a girl. It was said that she was a great pet of Puccini and his favourite ' Butterfly '.

Once, to my amazement, she sang the whole of the aria *One Fine Day* for Miss Whelan (the manageress) and myself in the downstairs lounge of the Monument Cafe in Grafton Street. It was a thrilling experience and, even after so many years, I find it hard to convince myself that it really took place. Ethereal happenings did not seem to belong in such mundane surroundings—but she would not have agreed with me there.

Opera is a Tower of Babel in which the Italian tongue predominates. While Margaret Burke Sheridan spoke—or rather sang (for she was a thrush really)—in the five or six languages in which *divas* communicate—hopping from one linguistic branch to another—her shapely hands sculpted the missing parts of the conversation. She had lost little of her legendary beauty at this time (it was said that one of her unrequited lovers had thrown himself from the top floor of the Savoy Hotel in London) so that physical proximity with her radiant presence was enough to make a green young man giddy. Her autumnal beauty is captured in a pastel also by Genaro, dated 1943, in the Gaiety Theatre in Dublin.

Sean O'Sullivan, the painter, was another of my characters. He was an outstanding portrait draughtsman rather than a painter. These gifts aside, he was an astounding personality. He spoke French and Irish as fluently as he spoke English. He had known Joyce well in the Paris of the 'thirties. He was a superb conversationalist and raconteur. As a painter he made it his business to record every person of prominence on the Irish scene during his period. If commissions were not available, he would resort to such steps as persuading a distillery to use reproductions of his drawings of current personalities on their calendars. The accumulation of his recorded observations would fill a large gallery, but we are fortunate in having a very representative display of his portraits in the National Gallery of Ireland. He had an anecdote to relate concerning every poet, politician, businessman, church man or celebrity that ever sat for him. These tales had the quality that was also to be found in his drawings—trenchant observation and an economy of means.

Sean was built on a generous scale. He had kept his amplitude within bounds in earlier years by fencing and the like, but now his frontiers were advancing in many directions at once. He liked drinking or, more properly, getting drunk. He loved to indulge in the pantomime of inebriation—it gave such licence to a man who was otherwise rather inhibited.

There was something marvellously orotund in the way he could utter outrageous sentiments. 'Madam, I wish to paint you because you have a bottom like a *meringue'*, was the answer he gave, loud and rumblingly clear in a crowded Jammet's (the best restaurant this side of the Atlantic from the fall of France to the Liberation) when a nettled dowager demanded to know why he persisted in asking her to pose for him.

One of his favourite things was to say (confidentially, as it were) to those persons of all too evident propriety: 'We *are* the people our mothers warned us against.' Whenever two or three were gathered together in the name of literature, he would boom: 'Dublin is a city of spoiled Prousts'—a remark which had originated with Seumas O'Sullivan (no relation, Seumas O'Sullivan was the *nom-de-plume* of James Starkey), the first editor of *The Dublin Magazine*, who had said: 'There are hordes of critics eager to give birth. But it is a phantom pregnancy. Nothing is born.'

Sean stopped me in the street one day. The following exchange took place:

'I say, Ryan, I've been reading that magazine of yours—
Envoy . . .'
(Me) 'Oh.'
'Very good thing there by that chap Cronin. Poem about
his father.'
(Me) 'Ah, yes.'
'He's got the what-yar-may-call-it . . .'
   (His chubby hands groped in air for the lost words)
'He's got, yes, the lyric . . . DAMN! . . . what's the
word . . ??'
   (He clicked the fingers of both hands in frustration, like a
   man trying to catch a waiter's attention)
(Me) 'Thing?'
'Fing . . . That's it. The lyric FING. G'bye.'

He had painted portraits of my father (a Senator and a
founding father), two of my sisters and my younger brother.
It soon came to my turn. He told me a complicated story about
how the direct descendant of 'Kelly the Boy from Killane'
was in financial straits and how Val Vousden, a great
traditional entertainer, and a friend and colleague of the immortal Percy French, was trying to dig up some gold for him.
Sean's contribution to the fund would be to donate the fee I
would be paying him for the portrait commission. It was a
roundabout way of having one's portrait solicited but perhaps
only for that it might never have been done and, besides, the
fee was modest. I am glad now I have it to look at in my evening years. One should never have oneself portrayed except in
youth. If a lifetime were a day (as in the case of the butterfly)
this portrait of me was drawn at about half past ten of a fine
morning. With only a few clouds on the horizon, it would
surely be a long, not to say, glorious day . . .
Certain people are given the rank of 'characters' by
universal acclaim—and not necessarily by any outstanding
eccentricities. It is as though there is an unspoken agreement

between character and audience on the point. In the field of commerce, Denis Guiney, or 'Dinny' as he was popularly known, was as much talked about as a major football star is today. He had 'come up' from remotest Kerry, taken a job as a drapery assistant and wound up by owning Clerys, one of the largest department stores in Ireland. Dinny had passed the Dublin test and was accepted as one of their characters.

He was famous for his rock-bottom sales. His merchandise had a more utilitarian than exotic appeal, but was always good value. Once, a shopper in the free-for-all scrummage of a January fur sale emerged somewhat roughed-up bearing a fairly presentable coat of dyed rabbit pelt for the not inordinate sum of £5. Later, when she brought it to a furrier to have the sleeves altered, he remarked that it seemed a pity to be cutting up a mink of such rare quality. Then she went to an insurance assessor to have it valued. Without hesitation he put a figure of £1,500 on the coat.

But she was an honest woman and could not live with her windfall, however innocently she had come by it. She brought it back to Dinny and told him the true value of it.

'Yerra, ma'am', said he, 'I bought up the entire contents of a warehouse of fur coats in Liverpool for £20,000. I sold out the whole lot at the sale for £25,000, giving myself a mark-up of 25 per cent. I don't know, and I couldn't give a damn, what was in it; whether 'twas blue mink or tom cat 'tis all the wan to me. Good luck to ye—and well wear.'

Dinny owned a restaurant in his establishment—a modestly posh affair for a departmental store. It was an instant success. One day when I was having lunch there, Dinny came in to have a quick look to see that everything was all right. He must have spotted some old pal from the Kingdom, for the next moment he was conducting a conversation with him over my head and the whole length of the room:

'Begod, there you are, Pat, me sound man! Is de grub all right? Grand. Game ball! How's all in Cahirciveen? Man yourself. See ya.'

Joe McGrath was, by governmental appointment, the first Free State millionaire. Having had the franchise of the Irish Hospital Sweepstakes given to him, he was in the position of a man who is given a colour offset lithographic machine by the authorities with the injunction : ' Now go ahead and print all the five pound notes you need.'

He had what the masses like in their millionaires. He was large and bulky, smoked big cigars, wore an outrageous white golf cap, two-tone shoes, travelled in a chauffeur-driven Rolls-Royce, lived in a great house, kept strings of racehorses, capturing all the great prizes like the Derby and the St Leger. He had been an IRA leader and a cabinet minister in Cosgrave's first Dáil, so he was indeed a *rara avis;* a Catholic republican millionaire on handshaking terms with royalty, within the life-span of people who remembered the great Famine and the *Times* newspaper foreseeing that we might shortly expect an Irishman on the banks of the Shannon to be as rare a creature as a Red Indian on the banks of the Hudson.

For those who liked the truly flamboyant, there was Jack Doyle. Against the grey austerities of the times he stood out like a peacock. A sometime contender for the world heavy-weight title, he had possessed as a young man in the Brigade of Guards all the physical requirements to fill that role—but his heart was in such exotica as sharing baths of champagne with Barbara Dodge, not in the fighting game. He had a pleasant tenor voice as well and for a time his ambition was to be a sort of combination of two other Irishmen—Gene Tunney and John McCormack.

As for the first of these dreams, it ended like a sack of potatoes on the canvas in Madison Square Garden when Buddy Baer eliminated his pretentions in this field for good and all. But he had made money and was now spending it like it was going to go out of fashion—to be Damon Runyonesque about it. With his dazzling wife, the Mexican actress, Movita (later to marry Marlon Brando), he cut a figure with his check suits, canary waist-coats, wild black locks of hair, wads of fivers, pocketfuls of Coronas, and huge rings. Inevitably, he

E

was the darling of the mob, and no race meeting or party was complete without him.

And he still had that tenor voice—however slight it may have been. The memory of Jack Doyle and Movita singing the ' Indian Love Call ' from *Rose Marie* on the vast stage of the now vanished Theatre Royal in Hawkins Street—a mammoth vaudeville theatre which rivalled in size and gaudiness the Roxy in Manhattan (on which it was modelled, down to the detail of having Royalettes—a Hibernian equivalent of the leggy Rockettes)—is a technicoloured memory of incredible vividness of something which was, for my then unsated eyes, larger than life itself.

7

In the Joyce Country

I made the pilgrimage,
In the Bloomsday swelter,
From the Martello tower
To the cabby's shelter.

Patrick Kavanagh: *Who killed James Joyce?*

There was an epitaph in those days, so frequently used by the men engaged in writing the hagiography of the saints of the early Irish language revival, that the phrase won from Myles na gCopaleen the special assay, or hall-mark, that the great man reserved for impeccable cliché. It ran somewhat like this: 'He spoke it (the *Irish*) at a time when it was neither popular nor profitable.' It was a cliché with a vengeance, and so beloved of these unctuous hacks, that it would still be unblushingly presented years after Myles had slaughtered it with mockery, so that for most of us, on hearing it again, the best we could do to conceal our amusement was the timely positioning of a pensive palm athwart the lower face.

So, to give the old thing another airing, let me say that I was a Joycean (or Joyce-man) when it was neither profitable nor popular. A recurring adolescent illness (bronchitis), which frequently visited and very nearly laid me low on two occasions, was, perhaps, the cause of my reading *Ulysses* at the comparatively early age of seventeen. It was a book I had heard of vaguely, because in ' with it ' Rathgar of the nineteen-thirties the smart thing was to smuggle it in wrapped in the dust jacket of Mrs Beaton's Jam Making Recipes or some such fare. I had heard of it as a *succès de scandale* . . . but no more.

I read the great book during a prolonged bout of this

recurrent complaint, at a time when I was neither pressed for time nor compelled to read for any academic purpose, and when I was even innocent of the fact that to accomplish so formidable a deed as this would open the doors of a hundred mews in Baggotonia. And because *Ulysses* came to me clean and unencumbered, with no layers of pseudo-scholarship to contend with, while my mind was white, original and virginal, unseduced by the hindsight of others, and was able to entertain, with respect—but not too much awe, the almost preposterous assumptions that the book was making—the most hilarious, as far as I was concerned, being the tacit one that we were now engaged, inter alia, in folding up the route map of the English language, a chart we would not be needing these next several hundred years.

Best of all, it was about Dublin and there was I, with the whole thing happening around me, albeit forty years later. It seemed incredibly modern then, though it is an ageless book, and to the young that is terribly important. I felt about Dublin as the Flower People felt about the Haight-Ashbury scene in the mid-'sixties—this is where it's all at. And what other city ever got a book of such stature written about it? Nothing of Dublin was too humble for Joyce to recall —nothing too dull or commonplace. Our songs, our voices, as insignificant as the twitterings of the starlings on the trees in O'Connell Street, even when as hollow as St Paul's tinkling cymbals became, under his hand, glorious cadenzas, brilliant arpeggios and dreamy codas penned across this mighty score.

When the call to Joycean duty came I, an early convert, was at hand . . . but by then all the world was there before me, it seemed.

You might as well be out of the world as out of fashion. When the James Joyce Tower Society was founded in 1962, I was invited to be one of its honorary secretaries. (The other was Miss Dorothy Cole). The Society came into being because the old Martello Tower in Sandycove, county Dublin, thanks to Michael Scott, the Irish architect, on whose land the tower stood, agreed to allow it become a Joyce Museum. The tower itself is a squat edifice, much more like a foreshortened butter churn than the slender, elegant, 'round' towers which can be seen so often in Ireland and are almost emblematic of the country. No mediaeval structure this, to hold aloft from the grasping hands of marauding Danes, the Church's treasured plate and relics; these bluff forts were built to keep 'Boney' from landing on the Irish shore. Designed at the instigation of Prime Minister Pitt, when the imminence of the *Grande Armée* was very much a reality and the loyalty of the Irish helots no matter of automatic assumption, should ever the day of reckoning come. They were modelled, and hence named, after a tower in Corsica (by a Napoleonic coincidence) which the British had managed to take, but only after a sustained and blood-drenched assault, a few years earlier. This tower was on Cape Mortella, meaning 'wild myrtle' which grew round the tower itself.

These bastions strung along the shallow sandy coast from Shankill (near Bray, county Wicklow) to as far north as Portmarnock, a distance of about forty miles, were like a necklace of rough-hewn beads, worthy of Mars himself. Each is within cannon range (three miles) of the other. Their object was to cover all beaches or low lying shore against the storming by infantry, to bombard ships at sea, within their range, and provide enfilading fire in the event of encirclement. Alas (for this country), they were never used.

That they survived at all, and so well (most of them can be seen to this day) is because they were built to immense structural specifications. The walls, of Wicklow granite, are eight-foot thick, rounded and sloping inwards to deflect fire. The entrance, as in the mediaeval round towers, is a narrow slit ten feet above the ground. Originally, only a retractable rope ladder was used, but in our time an iron staircase replaced that. There was so much gunpowder stored in these towers that the gigantic key to the door was made of bronze to avoid sparks and consequent risk of ignition.

The Martello Tower in Sandycove, and this is typical, commanded the views that had made the locality as scenically famous as it was strategically vulnerable. It dominates the superb vista of Dublin Bay—a crescent comprising (from this point) Dun Laoghaire, Blackrock, Merrion, Sandymount, Ringsend, Poolbeg and Bull lighthouses, with the spires of the city beyond; Sutton, the hill of Howth, the Baily, the span of open sea over the Rosbeg and Kish banks to complete a circle with the Muglin rocks near Dalkey Island and as much of the Wicklow Mountains (but not Bray Head, as Joyce—in reverie—thought) and the Dublin foothills, as the eyes could care to feast upon.

Oliver St John Gogarty (Buck Mulligan in *Ulysses*), rented the tower, which had been converted to the arts of peace perhaps half a century earlier and was now an ideally situated, if somewhat bizarre, 'gentleman's residence'. Still the property of the original builders, Gogarty paid his yearly rent of £8 to the Secretary of State for War. (We, in turn, paid our rent to the Department of Defence of the Irish Republic.) He inveigled or 'talked' Joyce into sharing the accommodation with him. At an overall rent of about three shillings a week, there was just a chance of the young and improvident poet managing his third (there was another paying guest, Samuel Chenevix Trench, the Englishman Joyce calls 'Haines' in the book); this sum being a shilling approximately.

Because of the situation and the superb vistas, but more because Joyce uses it as the port from which that great, leaky ark of his sets out to immortal seas on 16 June 1904, it was chosen as the memorial, the museum, the place of pilgrimage. Nobody who has read the book can face the tower and not see 'Stately, plump Buck Mulligan', boldly lit against the awakening mountains, lift his shaving bowl to the risen sun, his yellow dressing gown billowing about him in 'the mild morning air', commencing the proceedings of the age-long day and setting the sacerdotal tone of it by chanting, with all the guilty delight of the lapsed Catholic student that he was, the opening lines of the Mass: *Introibo ad altare Dei*.

Here then on 16 June 1962 we planted Joyce's banner on this

citadel. It was to mark the official opening of the tower. Sylvia Beach, Joyce's benefactress and publisher and, as such, midwife to so much of his literary output, travelled from Paris for the occasion. We had chosen the Milesian flag, the flag of Munster, Joyce's father's native province, the flag the Citizen waxed so warmly upon, rather than the Irish tricolour, which would have been an anachronism, one that had scarcely been adopted, even by the 'underground' movements in his day. This flag, which is three golden crowns on a field of St Patrick's blue, looked fittingly splendid as Sylvia Beach hauled it skywards as I fed it up to her, on the gunrest under the battlements, on that fine June day. There were clear skies and enough of a summer breeze to keel the racing yachts over, as they clawed around the mark off the nearby bathing cove.

FORTY FOOT GENTLEMEN ONLY, it said, on a board leading to this place of masculine ablutions (suggesting that a rival to the Giant's Causeway might lie beyond), while below us bobbed the heads of the assorted cognoscenti of several continents.

In the midst of her endeavours, a crumpled note, which had come up the winding stair from the tower's garrison quarters, addressed to Miss Beach, was pressed on me and by me handed to her. It read, simply: 'Back *Throwaway* in the 3.30. B. Behan.' *Throwaway* is the horse that won the Ascot Gold Cup, on the first Bloomsday, and the 'tip' which Bloom kept inadvertently giving or worse, *not* giving, and which very nearly led to his quietus at the hands of the Citizen in Barney Kiernan's pub in Little Britain Street. B. Behan is self-explanatory; he was down there somewhere in that seething, intellectual throng, but nearer the booze than most.

I also had charge, that day, of the bar. Unfortunately, not being Boyle Roche's bird, I couldn't be in two places at one time, so that large quantities of Powers Gold Label and John Jameson's Ten Year Old, found its way into the craws of other strange and completely unauthorized birds. However, gatecrashers notwithstanding, there was enough for all, so that in the tall grass surrounding the foot of the bastion and behind the flaps of the marquee, which we had put up for the liquid refreshments, could be seen, in repose, various scholarly and learned heads of many nations, not to say journalists and writers of world renown, as stoned as ever Ulysses' crew were in the land of the Lotus Eaters.

In the course of the following years, as secretary, I had occasion to meet many of the world's Joyceans, including the Bund President of Bavaria, who had learnt English and, incidentally, a love of Joyce, from his teacher, who had translated *Ulysses* and other Joyce books into German for the first time. Anybody who thinks that an intimate practical experience of Joyce's Dublin is essential for the understanding of his great tome can take heart from the following conversation which took place between the Herr President and myself, as we were making a Bloomsday ' Pilgrimace '. Understand, he had never been in Dublin before, but it was my twenty-fifth tour of the Ulyssean Dublin, more or less, in the role of guide.

We were bound for Glasnevin cemetery, the large metropolitan Necropolis, grave of our heroes, pantheon of our gods—*croak* park. Glasnevin is the locale of the ' Hades ' episode in *Ulysses*. I was driving the Herr President thither. Passing Botanic Avenue and nearing Glasnevin, there was one of those awkward pauses. In a half-hearted attempt to revive the moribund dialogue, I mentioned that there had been a notorious murder on this road, namely the ' Childs ' murder, in which the accused had been the brother of the victim. Simon Dedalus had talked about it to Martin Cunningham in the horse cab, when the two were similarly bound for the interment of poor Paddy Dignam. I remarked that the deed had taken place in one of the houses, but that I was not absolutely certain which. ' Yes ', the President murmured, knowingly, ' the last one on the right.'

Afterwards, back at the tower, our tour done, he clasped my hand, looked gratefully at me and, with so much emotion that I feared he would break into song (there and then), whispered breathlessly, ' This is the day . . . *how do you say it*—that I will remember . . . .'

Another time I had a Japanese professor who had worked on one of the several translations (I have knowledge of three) into Japanese. He was a member of that Yeats Society of Japan and thought *Finnegans Wake,* on the whole, fairly easy going. But then, he was the sort who might well have thought translating Kant's *The Critique of Pure Reason* into Upper-Urdu, child's play.

Anthony Burgess, author and etymologist extraordinary, told me that he had rendered *Ulysses* into Malaysian, but that he had encountered the same hurdle that has confronted and confounded would-be Gaelic translators—there is no word, in either language, it seems, for the expression of affirmation, ' yes ', the word which is crucial to the end of Molly's soliloquy. That Burgess jumped the hurdle eventually I have no doubt, but we, the Gaels, can get no nearer to that most vapid of words than *seadh*, which means, literally, ' it is so ' or ' so be it '. Nothing like the real thing by any manner or means. Mmmm . . . Yes . . .

I have heard more learned discourses on and about Joyce and all his works and pomps (some of them of such excruciating abstruseness as to make the mind wince), than the maître himself had hot dinners. (Well . . . in *Maxims*). I have had, in my official capacity, to attend seminars and summer schools devoted to Joyceana and often wondered how the English faculties, indeed the very language, survived until the advent of Shem the Penman. Truly, the groves of academe must have rung hollow and fretted for the day when that master punster (' germ's choice ') and linguistic prankster, would undo his satchel of scrabble in their schoolmarmish midst, bequeathing in that act a legacy of semantic conjuring tricks to keep them happy and gainfully employed for the rest of their days, and their students happily bewildered.

PART TWO

The Personalities

8

The Home and Colonial Boy

Youth inflicts the mortal wound
which age comes too late to heal.
Arland Ussher

When somebody enters your life for the first time, the initial image is imprecise—blurred. It takes time for the details to achieve focus. After all, it has yet to be established whether, in fact, the object is coming or going. For all we know it might, like a star, be receding. For that reason it is easier to remember when you *last* saw your father than when you first saw him.

While I am hazy as to the exact time I first met Brendan Behan (though I am sure that it was sometime late in 1943), I have no doubt as to the location—it was Des MacNamara's flat on the top floor of the Monument Cafe at 39 Grafton Street. Mac ran a sort of non-stop, Fabian *salon* in these premises from 1944 to 1948. I say non-stop because the pad was open to all-comers, quite literally, morning, noon and night. Mac was a gifted sculptor whose speciality was *papier-maché*. His one-room-studio-cum-bed-sitter was shared with his wife Beverly and some cats. Mac worked all day producing puppets, masks, stage props, window-models, even costume jewellery from this protean goo—indeed I still retain a door-knocker in the shape of Roger Casement's head (' the ghost of Roger Casement is knocking on the door. . . ') which, though of paper, has the consistency of cast-iron. It has been much coveted.

Mac cherished the company of writers, musicians, poets, artists or, lacking these avocations, the bizarre, the unorthodox or the innocent visionary. He could (and did) hold lengthy conversations on every imaginable topic with an unending stream of visitors, comprising loafers, itinerants, even celebrities. I remember T.H. White, whose book, *The Once and Future King,* became the musical *Camelot,* as a frequent caller and Erwin Schroedinger, the refugee from Nazi Germany—to whom de Valera had given sanctuary in the Institute for Advanced Studies. Schroedinger was a colleague of Einstein's who had expressed the theory of relativity for the first time in mathematical formulae, his hobby was weaving tapestry and he referred to himself as 'a naïve physicist'. E.J. Moeran, the Irish composer, was a frequent visitor.

Informal meals were eaten throughout the day and night, as a large black kettle always hung suspended over the turf fire in the corner. The Macs were true vegetarians—even excluding fish and eggs from their diet. One, therefore, would be likely to get a large, fresh hunk of vienna roll smothered in scallions, tomatoes and cheese, chased down with a mug of strong tea. The Macs were humane, as well as sophisticated, and knew that it would be unfair to extend their cult of vegetarianism to their room-mates of the feline category. To this end, meat, in the form of rib steak, was provided regularly for the cats.

It was after Brendan's Borstal and Curragh internment camp period but before the Walton Jail, Liverpool, days. I think he was actually on the run at the time, for he arrived and departed by night, although he sometimes slept there too—there was a spare bed of some description which he used.

He was about twenty years old. Good looking too, by any standards, especially with that shock of curly hair. He could have done with a few more inches in height, perhaps. Also his But he had sparkling eyes and very fine, even teeth, of which hands and feet were diminutive considering his over-all bulk. he was inordinately proud. The only appendage that accompanied him *everywhere* was the tooth-brush in his upper pocket. (Alas for the teeth—the butt of an automatic was to smash them out some years later in a brawl that was as ugly as it was futile; being neither founded on political conviction nor gainful crime). He was reasonably trim but possessed of one of those bodies that seem to yearn for weight.

Dionysian in his appetites even at this early age, his meals were orgiastic affairs of uninhibited recklessness, where pints and porter-house steaks would be lowered away to a band playing. Indeed, in the Behan household in Kildare Road, it was not unusual to find a galvanized bathtub, such as were once used for bathing children, full of a simmering mass of Irish stew in which it was likely an entire chicken might be found floating—or a sheep's head! With his father and four of the sons all out working as house painters, good money was coming in at last and all was possible. The fame of *Chez* Behan spread and even Patrick Kavanagh made a pilgrimage there to partake of the fabulous fare about which he had heard so much.

Predictably, the all-vegetarian MacNamara menu was not really his dish, though he discreetly kept his dislike of this ' rabbit food ' (as he called it) to himself, even reasoning that it was ' intellectual ' fodder and, as such, likely to be good for the brain.

One night when the MacNamaras were out visiting, they left Brendan to hold the fort against their return but, more importantly, to feed the cats. I was pottering about my own studio, which was next door, when my attention was distracted by an attractive smell of cooking coming from the Mac's residence. Deciding to investigate, I entered the room only to find ' your man ' frying a large juicy steak for the cats. He was turning it when I came in and, as it sizzled afresh, great wafts of unbearably succulent aromas filled the room. The cats arched their backs and purred . . .

' Christ ', gasped Brendan, ' God forgive me, I can't help it.' With that he did his best to push the entire steak into his mouth. Loud and prolonged screams issued from the demented tabbies.

' God's teeth ', I cried, ' what are they going to say when they come back and find you've eaten the cats' meat? '

' They won't know ', he mumbled between half masticated mouthfuls, ' c-cats c-can't t-t-talk ', (he was using the Behan stutter I was to get to know so well).

' They *will* know, because these cats cry when they're not fed. In fact, they set up an infernal din ' I argued.

' — it, you're right ', he mumbled apprehensively. Jaysus, do you think we could stuff radishes or scallions into them? '

' Not a chance ', I said, ' they're true carnivora.'

' What's that when it's at home? '

' Flesh eating mammals ', I replied.

Just then we heard the MacNamaras clambering up the stairs.

' Don't say a word ', he pleaded.

He had obviously had an inspiration, for without further ado he caught hold of the cats and, in turn, pressed each protesting muzzle into the melted dripping in the pan.

' What's the matter, little dears? ' asked Bev, confronted with the sight of the three cats and the sound of their lamentations—a woeful threnody.

' Did you feed them at all, Brendan? ' she asked suspiciously.

' Jaysus ', said he, ' can't you see the bastards lickin' their chops? ' and so they were. His stratagem had worked, for no matter how they complained, the irrefutable fact was there for all to see; they were plastered with fat and dripping!

' Good gracious ', said Bev, ' there was a good pound of meat in that.'

'Yerrah ', complained Brendan piously, between burps, ' there's no plasin' some bastards.'

Hitler and Behan were both unfulfilled house painters. Destiny had bigger plans for them—though, as events were to show, not necessarily better. Brendan, like all his brothers and his father learnt the trade of painter, which included a spell at the ' tech '. The daddy, Stephen, was president of the Irish Painters' and Decorators' Union which, of course, was a help

when it came to getting jobs. I remember an occasion when
Brendan was painting the Gaiety Theatre. I was strolling
down South King Street when he came bounding out through
the swing doors in his white overalls which were, like Joseph's
coat, of divers colours. Something was amusing him vastly.
' For Jaysus ' sake come here till I tell you, he chortled while
at the same time more or less aiming me into McArdle's pub
across the way. It seems that there was rehearsal of Terence
Rattigan's *The Winslow Boy* in progress and that he was up in
the flies—supposedly painting. The infant prodigy playing the
title role was behaving as child stars are expected to behave
and therefore giving everybody concerned a very hard time.
Brendan from his lofty eyrie manoeuvred himself into a handy
position directly above the prodigy and was able to allow the
contents of a gallon tin of white primer to descend and
envelop the head of the insufferable child. I am aware that he
varies the telling of this story in *Confessions of an Irish Rebel*
but this is how I remember getting it from him at the time,
immediately after the event.

Again I recall that my brother Paddy asked him to paint the
name of his firm (Ryan & Co.) on the door of his office.
Brendan painted it in Roman capitals with gold leaf and
shadow. All was middling-good except the N which was
upside down. The technical name in the trade for this work
was ' writing ' (hence ' sign writing '). One day I met an old
crony and fellow committee man of Stephen's in the Painters'
and Decorators', called Pa O'Toole. I asked him did he know
the Behan boys. He thought he did. He wasn't sure about
Brendan because he had spent so much time in the nick that
he wasn't all that well known in the trade. To make it easier
to distinguish him and because he had already had some small
pieces in Irish published, I referred to him as ' Brendan, you
know, the writer.' ' The writer?' he queried in surprise.
' There's only one writer in that family and that's the father,
Stephen. Did you ever see the sign for Guinness he done up
there on the gable over Slattery's in Phibsboro? Them letters

is seven foot high. And the pint he drew beside it, with the shine down the side and the big foamy head? Now that's writing. No . . . Stephen was the only one ever wrut in that family.'

Once Freddie May, the composer, gave both of us complimentary tickets to a performance of the opera *Pelias et Melisande.* We were, perhaps, too young fully to enjoy its exquisite felicities, for presently Brendan grew restive. He leaned back on his plush seat the better to peer into the recesses of the rococo ceiling. At last he found what he was seeking. ' Look ', be whispered urgently, stabbing chubby fingers upwards, ' between them fat, flying babies up there—that patch on Orpheus' arse—I was supposed to have washed that down. Ha! Ha! Jaysus . . .' Sure enough a rectangle of darker hue showed through the flights of the *putti* and the cavorting gods. A dismounted horse-Protestant just in front of him, not sharing his enthusiasm for unwashed ceiling allegories, pinned him to his seat with her opera glasses and silenced him with a vice-regal ' ssshhhhhh . . .'

Brendan brought me his first short story when I was editor of *Envoy*. It was called *A Woman of No Standing*. As a piece of writing it is as good as anything else he ever wrote; some think it his best individual piece. It has freshness, compassion and humour. My office, which was under Mac's old studio, which he had relinquished, had now become the casual meeting place for the Grafton Street boulevardiers and the MacDaidian intelligentsia. Brendan would come in for a fag or the ' lend of a loan' of a half note, or any other reason why. But this was his first professional appearance as you might say. The full span of his creative career only bridged the years 1950-1960, just ten years. It is not all that surprising that this, his first piece, should be as good as his later work. *Borstal Boy*, his acknowledged *chef d'oeuvre,* was itself partly finished at that time because he actually offered me a whole wad of it— though it was too late for publication, the last number of *Envoy* had gone to press. He wasn't sure what to call it but had provisionally dubbed it *Another Twisting Of The Rope*. I suggested *Bridewell Revisited*, a title which he was quite enthusiastic about. However, when it did see the light of the publishing day, it was under the bland and un-inventive title of *Borstal Boy*, a title which, no doubt, the pass B.A. ' reader ' who read it for his publisher, bearing in mind the possibilities of a *News of the World* readership, had thought terribly swinging.

In 1965 while searching through the old archives of *Envoy*, Anthony Cronin and myself found the manuscript. Cronin was the first to spot it, recognizing it from the actual physical shape it had assumed after months of close proximity (in the inside pocket) with the Behan anatomy, when he had hawked it from pillar to post. Written on it in his own hand was ' *A bit I'm not ashamed of; the title supplied by John Ryan for whom my affection is tenacious, invincible and reckless.*'

Sometime in 1952, a friend of mine who was then working as a photographer on the long vanished but then ever-so-trendy *Picture Post* and who wished to be rid of at least some of the austerities of post-war London (the puritan Chancellor, Sir Stafford Cripps—better known to his victims as Sir Stifford Crapps—had decided that the nation go into sackcloth and ashes for at least a decade to atone for winning the war) if it were only for a week, asked me if there was anything stirring in Dublin in the way of a story that would furnish him with the necessary excuse to come over for a paid holiday.

I told him that it was not a time of momentuous happenings in Ireland. However, I eventually came up with a story which I thought might just do. There was a bizarre young man of Rabelaisian proclivities who had spent, intermittently, the years since he was sixteen in various prisons for the cause of the Republic. I had recently published his first short story. Amongst other things, I had seen him float down the river Seine with a bottle of champagne which he was, at the same time, consuming with considerable expertise. Dan Farson (for he was the friend) took photographs and I wrote

the article. A new editor of *Picture Post* (the editorial casualty
rate at the time was about one a week) turned down the
whole thing on the grounds that Behan was unknown and of
no interest anyway. As we had been commissioned we were
paid. The article and pictures subsequently appeared in a
New Zealand illustrated magazine. That was the first time
that Brendan appeared in the full glare of the public stage.
It was not to be the last time. I often wonder what that same
editor thought in the subsequent ten years as the Behan
legend blazed out across the globe igniting a thousand head-
lines.

Like myself, he was born under the sign of Aquarius. No
wonder then that he was so well suited to the liquid world.
He could surround a bottle of whiskey more happily than any
man I knew. Like François Rabelais (to whom he bore more
than a superficial resemblance) he might as truly have said
' I drink for the thirst to come.' Equally he liked to sub-
merge himself in the fluid element. We used to go to the
Forty Foot bathing place and it was there that Farson took
some of his most memorable photographs of Behan delight-
edly wallowing in the sea, true as a turtle, or recumbent on
the shore, like a basking shark. One morning, as he was
dressing there, he remarked to a priest, who was a daily
swimmer. ' You know, father, after this early dip I really
believe I've earned my breakfus.' ' But of course ', the priest
replied. ' Aye ', said Brendan, rubbing his hands in anticipa-
tion, ' a large brandy and a plateful of benzedrine.'

When I had the yacht, ' Southern Cross ', Beatrice and he
used to come out sailing in Dublin Bay. His pleasure was to
sit in the stern (usually blocking all approaches to the tiller)
and spin for mackerel. Usually the boat, even in light airs,
was too fast, a characteristic which was the subject of much
fluent cursing on his part. ' The only thing you can catch
from this feckin' thing ', he would say, ' is a feckin' submarine.' Despite this, we always had a bottle or two of red
wine below decks so that all our voyages had auspicious
endings.

After the publication of Ulick O'Connor's biography of Brendan there was much righteous indignation, rending of garments and general foaming at the mouth because of the suggestion that he had been somewhat homosexually inclined. The then chief of staff of the IRA, Cathal Goulding had written a bellicose ' review ' of the book in *Hibernia* which was little short of a declaration of war on the book's author. Some of the tension was taken out of the situation by a heading in one of the Sunday papers which brought the thing back to its comic-opera proportions. It ran : ' Quare Fella— Queer? Query '. As one who knew him well (but not *all that well,* I hasten to add!) I can only relate that he made no great bones about the matter to his friends. His was a voracious sexual appetite and in Dublin vernacular of the time ' would get up on the back of the Drimnagh bus! '

I think that even apart from the years of enforced confinement with other men, he might have considered homosexuality as simply another tasty morsel or savoury on the *smorgasbord* of the Bohemian running buffet. But only as ' afters ' so to speak, following the main course. Booze, as always took precedence over all; this was the one subject about which he was neither lighthearted or irreverent. The definition of an Irish ' queer ' is supposed to be ' a man that prefers women to drink '. He certainly did not come into that category. He was openly ribald on the subject, just as he was derisive and blasphemous about most of the things that ignorance wraps in a cocoon of modesty and piety. He was vastly ahead of his comrades in intellectual stature, being, in the main, free of hypocrisy and humbug. After the publication of O'Connor's book, they wanted to give the impression of loyal friends rushing, posthumously, to the defence of their calumniated pal. All they succeeded in doing was to spell out their own distinctively bourgeois *mores* as they struggled to drag him down to their suburban level. He had faults, but intellectual dishonesty was not one of them.

It was I who introduced Brendan to Eddie Chapman. We met accidentally at Dublin Airport, casually introducing our-

selves over a drink in the bar—we were travelling by air and
so had time to spare. I cannot imagine such a meeting in the
soulless enormity of the present complex but in those days it
was quite an intimate place with nothing but the comings and
goings of a few DC3's to bother the management and a daily
passenger turnover that the belly of a jumbo airliner could now
swallow without any sign of indigestion.

It turned out that this Eddie Chapman was a famous safe-
cracking expert who in pre-war years had specialized in
' doing ' Odeon Cinemas. He had worked his way through
every one of the multitudinous branches of this organization
in the United Kingdom from the Mull of Kintyre to the
Channel Islands. He was aided in his scheme in that they had
all been designed by the same architect who, being no Mies
van der Rohe, was content to let the same plan serve for all.
Eddie could walk in with a blindfold on him and reach out
and infallibly touch the safe—useful when working in the
pitch dark.

Nemesis caught up with him on the Channel Islands, however, just when there were no more Odeons left to lay his
burglarious hands on, and there he was sentenced to many
years in prison. But hope in the shape of the Wehrmacht lay
just beyond the horizon. When the Germans invaded Alderney
in the summer of 1940 they did a little deal with Eddie,
whereby he was ' sprung ' on condition that he teamed up with
the Nazi spy organization.

He was trained by them in Berlin mainly in the complex
art of sabotage. In time he was parachuted into England with
a radio transmitter, a quantity of gelignite and a very large sum
in genuine Bank of England notes. The bulk of these he buried
beneath a tree ' somewhere in England ' to await the outbreak
of peace and his own happy return. He then gave himself up to
the nearest police. British Intelligence immediately grasped
the importance of his potential so he agreed to continue acting
as a German agent while being in fact one of their own on
condition that the rest of his sentence be struck from the rolls.

During the war he made several trips to and from England to the continent, departing by German submarine, and returning by parachute (with British MI5 shepherding him like a broody hen, her chick all the time) and staging acts of ' sabotage ' that he was supposed to have pulled off. One of his best deceptions was to radio back to Germany false information regarding the location of V1 and V2 bombs when they struck, which is the main reason why so many fell on the garden suburbs and not the port or industrial sector of London.

Eventually the Germans did get wise to him and he was awaiting the end in a concentration camp when once more an army came to the rescue—this time the liberating American one. The Germans had given him the Iron Cross first class but all he got from the Imperial Majesty (not counting the free pardon of course) was a hundred pound fine for contravening the Official Secrets Act *after the war,* by publishing a brief memoir in the magazine *Lilliput.*

By the time I introduced them (circa 1948) Eddie had acquired a small freighter, the *Sir James,* a vessel of some four hundred tons which was then plying the trade routes of the Irish sea. What cargoes she carried or from whence and to whom I never did discover. Eddie had a manner about him which discouraged such enquiries. When he smiled, gold wisdom teeth flashed on either side of his mouth but his eyes never smiled. There are some questions best left unasked.

At my instigation he was kind enough to sign Brendan on as (the Lord forgive me) an ' able-bodied ' seaman. For about six months they roamed the seas on many divers mercantile enterprises, and strange things befell them. They even managed to find a brothel in the sea port of Drogheda which they had reckoned to be as unlikely as finding one in Vatican City. It was of the stay-at-home and do-it-yourself variety being managed and staffed by a mother and her five daughters.

One day Eddie asked Brendan to paint the masts, reasoning that he must have some expertise at least in this field. Brendan proceeded to paint the mast upwards from the base to the top, or to be more nautical about it, from the heel to the truck. This ensured that when he made any of his frequent descents during the operations (be it for jar or pee) he must do so by slithering down a greasy pole which liberally plastered him with marine paint of the consistency of raspberry jam. Eddie pointed out that the correct procedure was to have yourself hoisted aloft on a bosun's chair to the truck and to paint as you lowered yourself down. His answer was to tell Eddie not to teach his grandmother how to suck eggs and to stick to navigating the leaky old hooker even though he knew — all about that too.

By the middle-'fifties Brendan Behan had become almost as infamous as the other B.B. of the mid-century—Brigitte Bardot. And as big a bore, not a few would impiously add. It was hard to say which part of the fame that accreted to him was of his own manufacture, and which was simply mud from the Fleet Street ditch that had clung. He seemed to be wired up to the media; his umbilical—the telephone wire. He only had to drop his pants in Grafton Street, Dublin, for the teleprinters to cackle in Galveston, Texas, or Osaka, Japan.

When the box-office receipts flagged in the West End, he would quite seriously wonder whether the time had not arrived to awake the lethargic Albions once again. Without further ado, having established this, he would take a plane to London, get into a brawl or two, have himself barred from the theatre which was showing his own play, having rushed onto the stage and made a drunken speech.

The parallel of the sorcerer's apprentice irresistibly presents itself here. For the more he, the journalist's friend, provided free copy, particularly for the ' splutter ' press, the more it wanted and the more he was expected to perform. The trouble about this kind of ballyhoo is that the recipient begins to believe it himself. He began to act earnestly the role of drunk-in-ordinary to the British and American public—he could have added ' by Royal appointment ' after Princess Margaret had come to see *The Hostage* and all but fallen out of her seat at the joke about ' Vat 69 ' being the pope's telephone number;

a joke I myself heard at Kilashee, a preparatory school for Clongowes Wood, very nearly kicking out the tailboard of the cot I was sleeping in at the time.

The sad thing was that he was, without needing to lay on anything thick, a genuine wit and wag. There was an abundance of ' copy ' in what he said, more than enough to satisfy the needs of the most avaricious of journalists. You don't come across a man who can engage Groucho Marx, effortlessly, in repartee, every day of the week. Once in an elevator in a New York hotel, Groucho commenced some anecdote by saying ' I was making *A Night at the Opera* when . . .' Brendan at once intervened with : ' That's like Michelangelo saying, " I was doing the murals in the Sistine Chapel at the time . . . ." '

Another incident—the real comedy of which the press missed—being as usual, in pursuit of sensation rather than wit —was when he was flying by Air France from Paris to London. Shortly after departure, the 'plane was struck by lightning. Brendan who was in the jigs anyhow, reacted in fear-shaken fashion. Apprehensive of any further consequences, the pilot decided to return to Orly for the purposes of unloading Brendan. At the airport he made a speech from the ramp to the inevitable assembly of press; in his quite good French : ' Je suis préparé à mourir pour la France, si c'est necessaire, mais certainement pas pour l'Air France!' (I am prepared to die, if necessary for France—but not for Air France!)

This was taken to be an insult to the ' honour and dignity ' of France and, as a result, he was lodged in the ' cage ' that ubiquitous article of the French penal code that can be found in all police stations. There he spent the night with some Algerian Nationalists. Brendan entertained the company during the night with songs and ballads. At one point, a member of the gendarmerie, who had been trying to sleep, rattled the bars of the cage with his submachine gun, making the ominous comment: ' Regardez la mitraileuse '—(see the machine gun) to which Brendan replied, ' Je le vois : dommage que tu ne l'avais pas à la Ligne Maginôt.' (I see it. It's a pity you didn't have it on the Maginot line.) He told me the whole

story on our way to the Air France office in Westmoreland
Street in Dublin to collect the money owed to him for his
unused ticket. The papers simply proclaimed the fact that he
had been drunk and disorderly.

As the illness grew, the drinking increased; he was stupified
from both. I had dinner in Jim Downey's Steak House on
Eighth Avenue, New York, with Beatrice and himself one
evening in April 1963. ' You've come a long way from Mac's
studio in Grafton Street where you ate the cats' dinner ', I
observed. But he was too sick and tired even to smile. He just
sat there like a mound of blubber—or Orson Welles in the
last reels of *Citizen Kane*.

A myth that might well be exploded is the one that got a
universal airing immediately after his death, which is typical
of the kind of *smaltz* that infests the more yellow journalism
on such melancholy occasions: that was the one that seemed
to imply that it was the inconsiderateness of his friends that
had hastened his death. Nothing could be further from the
truth. A few things should be remembered: Behan, though
generous in many ways, (particularly to the really down-and-
out) was notoriously tight-fisted when it came to buying a
round in the company of his coevals—' slow on the draw ' as
they used to say in the vernacular. His taste ran to treble
brandies in these latter years. This exotic preference, coupled
with his unwillingness to return the compliments, didn't
greatly endear him to the Irish, who are very down-to-earth
when it comes to the mechanics of drinking. However elevated
they may become as a result of its consumption. At this time,
be it also remembered, he was also quite an appalling messer.
One would have to rifle the annals of Bacchus to find a more
determined nuisance in drink. If he wasn't falling on you and
spilling drinks over you, he was mauling your wife or girl
friend to the accompaniment of an unbroken dirge of truly
' foul ' language. He would punch and claw you if he felt
you weren't giving him one hundred per cent attention—not
the easiest thing to mime when you were hearing some story
you had heard a million times before. One day, when he was

not all that much advanced in alcoholicity, he felt the need to expose his genitals to a pub half-full of indifferent boozers. It was a depressing, though poignant, illustration of what Paul Valéry meant when he wrote: 'When one no longer knows what to do in order to astonish and survive, one offers one's *pudenda* to the public gaze.'

Once, in the Bailey, he vomited straight out onto the floor in mid-sentence, but completed it, nevertheless. He would empty a pub in about two minutes flat. I should know. I worked for one of the few from which he was not barred. Old friends fled when they saw him coming. Even the needy who depended on him for the odd drink began to dread him. One of the last of his 'minders', Eddie Whelan, a married man with children who was a paid drinking companion, told me how he would be dragged from bed at any old hour of the night, by Brendan, who would arrive in a taxi, to commence the day's marathon of drinking. 'People think I do well out of this', he confided, 'but I was making better money as a bricklayer. Pity to God I ever gave it up.'

Brendan and I dined once more that year. This time back in Dublin at the Bailey. It was a quiet afternoon and we were the only ones in the restaurant at the time. Anthony Cronin joined us. One of the waiters, Roy, had a transistor which was emitting signals that only he was able to interpret. Presently he volunteered the information that the sounds seemed to suggest that President Kennedy had been shot and killed in Dallas, Texas. Brendan started crying: 'He invited me to the reviewing stand for the inauguration', he mumbled. Then he called for a taxi. It was years afterwards that I heard that he had been driven straight to the American Embassy where he was one of the first to sign his name on the Book of Remembrance. Behan, the showman, was never slow in following up an event potentially favourable for publicity, however befuddled he was by alcohol.

His drinking, which was entirely self-inspired and self-motivated, had taken on epic proportions. He had passed from drinkard to drunkard to alcoholic and, finally, to dipsomaniac.

One day, on an impulse, he had withdrawn £500 from the bank, picked up an acquaintance, Philip Corley, with whom he had been out on the tiles the previous night, and with him, took a plane from Dublin Airport bound for America. Finding that there was no bar service on the Dublin-Shannon stage of the flight and noting that Corley had, in a hold-all, packed a bottle of after-shave lotion, he grabbed it, unscrewed the top, and swallowed the contents in one almighty draught. They refused to take him any further than Shannon.

I saw him from time to time during those last months. He would lope into the Bailey, more dead than alive. Sometimes he would simply stare. A photograph which was taken in an automatic ' photo booth ' at Amiens Street station a month or so before his death will give an idea of the terrible condition that had so rapidly overwhelmed him.

Oddly, he is least remembered for what he did for his country. As a young member of the Irish Resistance, he had freely sacrificed his youth for the ideal of a free and, he hoped, socialist, non-sectarian Ireland. While his contemporaries had their fling, he languished in British jails and Irish internment camps. Even as a boy, he had tried to enlist in the International Brigade in the Spanish Civil War. He came very close to the firing squad after the shooting incident at the 1916 Commemoration march to Glasnevin in 1943. He was not wanting in courage. Of all the writers, poets or painters of his generation, he was the only one who took up arms, literally, for the freedom of his country. If he was selfish and egotistical in other things—he was a completely committed patriot. What he did with utter unselfishness cannot be taken from him. The value of his literary estate may be argued, but not this. When he died, the IRA gave him a burial with all they could provide by way of full military honours—a guard of honour, an oration and after the mourners had departed, a furtive firing party at the grave.

An uncommonly mild day it was, that nineteenth day of March in the year of 1964. A surgical theatre in Dublin's

Meath Hospital. The patient is unconscious and breathing heavily. A tube enters his throat (a tracheotomy) beneath the ample, rounded chin; another, presumably for intravenous feeding, is connected to some part of the abdomen. A hand lies authoritatively across a generous chest—it is the pose that a politician might take after delivering a ponderous, postprandial cliché, anticipating a round of applause.

There is a Roman quality to the massive young head and the great mane of brown hair that tumbles rebelliously over the edge of the operating table. A large, well-proportioned frame, not unduly corpulent, covered in a soft unwrinkled skin that could have been a girl's (it is almost downy), which has now taken into its natural pigmentation a curious, lemon-coloured tinge.

The theatre is silent save for the barely audible scratchings of a pen as a worried-looking nurse makes notes in the day-book. A coloured house-surgeon—Pakistani perhaps—is darkly silhouetted against the window, a stethoscope nonchalantly swinging, pendulum-wise, between his knees. Muted, faraway city murmurings only emphasize the prevailing afternoon stillness. James Clarence Mangan, another poet, had died in this same hospital, young and destitute, a hundred years earlier. There is a sense of restfulness about the place, as though the outcome of some great struggle had been decided. Time itself seems to be dying and this, in turn, induces a torpid drowsiness. I feel like a swimmer effortlessly floating on the water of Lethe.

The breathing sound persists, relentlessly, like a metronome, while the stethoscope involuntarily keeps time. The only urgency is in that sound, the sound of the body's motor, itself part of an abandoned vehicle running out, on the last of its fuel. What signals the body's own computer must be sending forth now that the surgeons have thrown in their hand? Futile signals calling up spent reserves, urging exhausted components. Betrayed, the body lingers on death's threshold; more reluctant than the spirit to enter. . . .

As a gesture of farewell, I touch the hair of his head. My hand lingers, it is warm.

'*Ave atque vale*', I think. (It is difficult, in grief not to be rhetorical—even with oneself).

We leave the room and descend the stairs, Kathleen, Stephen and myself. Earlier they had called on me at the Bailey and asked me to take them to the hospital. This I did, thinking no more than that was required. Both, however, insisted that I accompany them all the way. I knew that Brendan's condition was terminal, that he was grossly cirr-hosed and I was loath on that account to appear as an idle spectator. I was relieved when I heard the hospital receptionist say that only members of the family could be allowed to see him, until they countered this by telling her that I was Rory Furlong—Kathleen's son by an earlier marriage and Brendan's own half-brother! Like it or not I now had to enact the role of her surrogate offspring. Later in the day the *real* Rory had trouble getting in himself, due to this earlier deception.

I remarked, limply, that Brendan looked rather well, apart from that yellow hue. He did, in fact. Death evidently takes a great weight off the mind, for what I saw in him, I have seen in others—the mocking erasure of the years, life's final prank, death's first joke—he looked positively young.

'He won't live beyond this afternoon, John, dear', his mother said quietly.

We made our way back to the Bailey. The clans had begun to gather and the drink to flow. A period of great conviviality, never long separated from death among the Irish, was now imminent. Only the final confirmation was required for the balloon to ascend in earnest. At six o'clock a 'phone call came from the Meath. Yes, all was well now. Brendan Behan had died peacefully. He had just turned forty. Kathleen was right.

Next morning, Muscovites, reaching for the samovar, read the news in *Pravda*. Less surprised, Brooklyn taxi-drivers learnt all about it in the *Daily News;* the private, deadly struggle in the Meath Hospital was done and the thin-spun life slit, irrevocably. In the moment of consummation, the intimacy and the urgency were both lost. This terrible silent event now balloons grotesquely into the banalities of the front page. . . . But time will take up the theme from here, will tone it down into history and, later, lovingly embroider it as legend.

9

The Lost Umbilical Chord

The Irish are not in a conspiracy to cheat the world by false representations of their countrymen. No, sir; the Irish are a fair people—they never speak well of one another.
Samuel Johnson (Boswell's *Life*)

Feel free to pick your own favourite from the innumerable stories that purport to give the origins of Eoin O'Mahony's (Eoin [the 'Pope'] O'Mahony, K.M., S.C. 1906-1971) unusual nickname. The one that has gained greatest currency is the one that, recalling his Cork childhood, has him answering the stock question that is put to children: — 'What are you going to be when you grow up?', not with the predictable 'engine driver' but the altogether more exotic 'Pope'.

O'Mahony was a distinguished pan-European Christian, a Knight of Malta and, deep down in his heart, a strolling aristocrat *manquée* from the courts of the Stuarts. His dream, quite seriously, would have been a united Irish monarchy, with 'Nicky' Gormanston (an Irish Catholic Lord and the premier viscount of the land) on the throne. Failing this the Reverend The O'Conor Don (the last direct descendant of the High Kings of Ireland) and a Jesuit, would have to be persuaded to forsake his vows and assume the lapsed monarchy. And yet he was more a radical humanist than anyone would guess. Sometime, someone will do this country and his memory the honour of producing a definitive 'life' of the Pope.

I worked with him on many causes—not always lost. We successfully fought together, for instance, on his Republican Prisoners' Release Committee and by prodigious effort (mostly his, I may say), secured the release of the IRA prisoners who

John Ryan strolling down Grafton Street in 1941—during the 'emergency'.

The McDaid's crowd setting out for the 'Catacombs' (circa 1949). Des MacNamara is on the extreme left while Gainor Crist (the 'Ginger Man') is third in from the left, standing.

J. P. Donleavy and Philip Wiseman, the producer, pictured outside the Gaiety Theatre the evening *The Ginger Man* was taken off. (Photograph: *The Irish Times*).

Under the title 'Dublin Culture', this cartoon by the New Zealand caricaturist Alan Reeve was published in the *Irish Times* in 1940. The setting is the back room of the Palace Bar in Fleet street. Those sketched are:—
BACK ROW (from left-hand corner): John P. Colbert (with pipe), G. H. Burrows, Francis MacManus, Maurice Walsh. (standing) Patrick Kavanagh. (centre back) Brian O'Nolan, Liam Redmond, Donagh MacDonagh. (standing) John Chichester. (seated, right-hand corner) Austin Clarke, Padraic Fallon, F. R. Higgins. MIDDLE ROW (from left): (standing with camera) Alec Newman. (seated, at table below camera) Ewart Milne, Lynn Doyle, Leslie Yodaiken, Roibeard O

Farachain, M. J. MacManus (in black hat). (standing) Tom, one of the barmen. Centre table (from left) R. C. Ferguson, Esmonde Little, R. M. Smyllie, Brinsley MacNamara. (below) William Conor. (looking at book) Seumas O'Sullivan. Right-hand table (at top) Cathal O'Shannon, Jerome Connor, David Sears. (at bottom) George Leitch, Desmond Rushton. BOTTOM ROW (from left): Alan Reeve (black suit and beard), G. J. C. Tynan-O'Mahony, A. J. Leventhal, Edward Sheehy. Centre table (front) Patrick O'Connor, Harry Kernoff, Sean O'Sullivan. Bottom (right) Jack, Sean and Mick.

John Ryan, Anthony Cronin, Brian O'Nolan, Patrick Kavanagh and Tom Joyce on Sandymount Strand, Bloomsday, 1954 (Photograph: *The Irish Times*).

Patrick Kavanagh and Brian O'Nolan at the Bailey, 1954. (Photograph: *The Irish Times*).

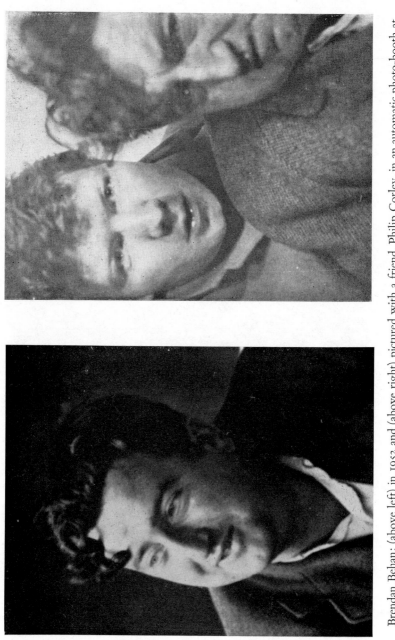

Brendan Behan: (above left) in 1952 and (above right) pictured with a friend, Philip Corley, in an automatic photo-booth at Amiens Street Station shortly before his death.

had been in jail since the 1939 bomb war in Britain, from a most reluctant Labour Home Secretary, Mr Chuter Ede, in 1947.

It was in the nature of the sort of man that the Pope was—an amalgam of philosopher, historian, romantic and artist, to lack pragmatism. I remember an occasion when Brendan Behan and two companions got themselves involved in an affray with the porters at the front gate of Trinity College. It seems they wished to make a short cut to Pearse Street via the university itself. The porters disputed what they considered to be their inalienable, not to say immemorial, rights of let and hindrance and the inevitable brawl ensued. All three were lodged in the Bridewell having been, as they say, ' busted '. I was approached for help and, realizing that the charges could be quite serious, sought out and found the Pope who was living in Trinity College at the time. He had some loose working arrangement with this institution whereby there was always a room and a bed available. To contact the Pope you either wrote to him at ' Front Gate, Trinity College ', or, surprisingly enough, the men's hairdressing salon in the Gresham Hotel. Many's a letter I had from him bearing the crest and address of that well-heeled Dublin hostelry.

But to resume : Brendan and his two companions, whom we will call, for the purpose of our tale, Carmichael and Daly, were severally and jointly charged with conduct likely to lead to a breach of the peace, insofar as they did attempt and indeed caused, actual bodily harm to three persons, to wit the porters at the front gate of Trinity College—they—meanwhile, being preoccupied with the execution of their duty.

All the parties duly assembled at Court No. 2, Morgan Place. The Pope—being a lawyer—had, needless to remark, presented himself, with no question of fees, to act for the defence. It was one of those open and closed sort of cases; you did it or you did not. The evidence that the defendants had done it was, alas, overwhelming. The best the Pope could do was to make a plea for leniency, based on the defendants' youth, fiery temperament and acute social consciousness.

G

His experience at the bar, more than likely, told him that all this would not cut much ice—but at least his prayer would not do much harm either. Meanwhile, he had discovered that one of the defendants had six children—a useful plea for mitigation should the worst come to the worst. Unfortunately, in the hurly-burly of the last-minute consultation with his clients, he got the names of two of the defendants mixed up and, instead of begging the court to be particularly clement to Carmichael, (the father of the six children), he addressed himself to the judge most movingly and eloquently on behalf of the un-married and childless Daly. The sum of the matter was that Behan and Carmichael got a month while Daly got a fort-night! Protests from the dock by Carmichael were sternly put down by the judge who threatened contempt of court if there were any further irregularities. There was not much else to be done about it. Brendan told me afterwards that the next time the Pope offered to defend him for riding a bicycle without a lamp at night, he would probably be hanged. On the other hand, he said, it would be churlish to refuse his well-inten-tioned offer.

An early conservationist—he was, I remember, A Man Of The Trees (do they still exist?), had a keen eye for natural and architectural felicities and was deeply concerned about the general deterioration of our environment. He played an im-portant role in the restoration of Daniel O'Connell's birthplace at Derrynane and also worked assiduously on behalf of the Irish Georgian Society.

Historian, patriot, humanitarian though he was, he will probably be best remembered as a genealogist. His radio series, 'Meet the Clans', which lasted for seven years on Radio Eireann and is, fortunately, still preserved on tape, is a marvellous compendium containing the exclusive story of our history as expressed by pedigree and lineage—here is a virtuoso, verbally expressing the whole racial memory—not just recalling great events or personages; the voice of the tribe as well as the Almanach de Gotha.

How many family trees the Pope could climb! I tagged

behind him on quite a few of these arboreous ascensions. One could almost hear the family branches breaking before his relentless clambering.

No other mortal brain could house the formidable assemblage of genealogical data that his did, so that although his chronicles would knock miles off a journey or keep company agog until the small hours, it was impossible to retain a thousandth part of all that priceless information, while the pawky wit (which ever kept tedium at bay) and the endless revelation of yet more family skeletons, rendered them, though unsuitable at the time for the printed page or the broadcast voice, cherished memories which, alas, our too fallible memories could not, in most cases, retain.

I have a fair recollection, however, of one of those genealogical discourses for which he was rightly famous. By some instinct or oddity (the Pope's own oddness was, perhaps, catching?) I resolved, this once, to take unobtrusive notes of his disclosures. Looking back, it occurs to me that I might have wanted to know how what he had to say would *read* by dawn's early light without, as I say, that plump, spherical accent, as ample, placid and adamant, indeed as liquid, as his own lovely Lee. Was it in fact, all some form of incantation— some dreamy Cork sorcery?

It was a bleak February in a bad year. I was stamping my feet on the platform at Kingsbridge station in Dublin and slapping my arms around my shoulders to keep some circulation going. Drifts of dirty snow, like spindrift on a gale-lashed sea, were coming down the tracks from the sheds at Inchicore. I was cursing the business that was sending me this perishing morning to our *ultima thule*, West Connacht, when I caught sight of the roly-poly figure approaching like a Galway hooker butting an Atlantic chop.

It was the Pope alright, led by his paunch, the striped legal trousers at half-mast and the King's Inns' close-buttoned jacket. He had no topcoat but a voluminous Trinity rugger scarf wound many times about his neck was holding its own against the blizzard.

Like myself, he was making the train journey to Galway—
had, in fact, arrangements to meet the Marquess of Sligo in
those parts. No doubt the many bursting manila folders which
his plump fingers were attempting to restrain from taking on
separate existences of their own related to this forthcoming
business with his Grace.

We managed to get a bottle of ' Winter's Tale ' (appro-
priately enough) sherry in the station bar, also ham sand-
wiches of some considerable antiquity which we found
reclining in coy superannuated repose beneath an unclear glass
dome. Thus fortified we proposed to survive the journey on
this unprecedented February day which, as we have noted, was
situated plumb and at the very fulcrum and nub of winter.
The only other occupants of our third-class carriage were a
priest, greatly advanced in years, thumbing his breviary (and
much fatigued, he told us, after a stormy crossing of the Irish
Sea the previous night) and a scrawny woman of the west with
a quick darting eye and knitting needle fingers, who was
resigned, evidently, to some insuperable woe.

The locomotive that drew the Galway train in those days
was that great iron mare, the Queen Maeve. By and by (after
much snorting, shuddering, belching and coughing), she put
her massive shoulders to the wheel and dragged an assortment
of rickety squealing carriages and goods waggons, protesting,
in her train.

But, inspired by her good example we pursued the Queen,
like dolphins in the wake of an ironclad. Chapelizod, Lucan,
Leixlip, Maynooth, Kilcock, Kinnegad, all fled past us while
her splendid white plume of smoke momentarily challenged
the scudding snowladen clouds.

Nothing escaped the Pope's attention and we were treated
to brief potted biographies, epitaphs, elegies, judgements and
prophecies concerning all those of rank, wealth or distinction,
sacred or profane, who dwelt or had dwelt on the onrushing
prospect either side of the permanent way.

Presently the Pope remarked on the vestigial remains of an
estate in the distance. A straggling avenue of forlorn lime

trees led to a wilderness of bramble and dead rhododendrons, from out of which a single charred finger of masonry probed the sullen, leaden sky as if to press the point that here once stood a notable mansion.

' Ah . . .', murmured the Pope, ' that must be Rathmogerly Castle. I knew it well. As a boy I once cycled all the way from Clongowes to see the azaleas in bloom—that was when the Plunkington-Foreshaws were living there. Lady Sarah was herself one of the Fitzroy-Plantagenets and noted for her *fêtes champêtres*. It is said that Earl Kitchener (of Khartoum) was attending one of these functions at the castle when he received the summons to assume the viceroyship of India, but that he was so overwhelmed by the occasion that he spilt his glass of champagne over the Countess of Cappawhite's muslin tea gown. She was then in her ninety-fifth year and had known Wordsworth as a young girl.' The mellifluous Cork cadences were now fairly cascading as the Pope worked up to his theme.

' The Foreshaws were a decent Catholic-Protestant, Anglo-Irish family. One of their forebears—a Dolan from Westport (who changed his name by deed-poll) was the midshipman on the *Victory* who translated Nelson's commands to the fore-topmen into Irish, because they were all native speakers from Cape Clear Island, with no English. The Plunkingtons were the natural issue of a liaison between Harry, first duke of Grafton, the illegitimate son of Charles the Second who fell at the siege of Cork, and an amorous adventure with Charlotte Albion whose family changed their name to Brython and whose motto was ' Facile Princeps ' (Indisputedly the First.)

' Lady Sarah's half-sister, Mildred, daughter of Plunkington's first wife, later to become the Dowager Duchess, had been the centrepiece of an extraordinary international scandal involving Sir Reginald Arbutus Knee-Capps, Her Imperial Majesty's rascally envoy to the Sublime Porte during the reign of the last Sultan of the Ottoman Empire, bar one. Tim Healy's brother Tom, a taciturn man most times, knew " Arby " Knee-Capps well and could be induced (given the necessary quantity of port) to expand upon his extraordinary misconduct during post-prandial revelries on the old Munster circuit. While she was his mistress in Constantinople, he had attempted to smuggle Mildred into the palace seraglio, a deal having been struck with the keeper, the Sublime Eunuch, to pass her on to the Sultan in exchange for one of the Exhalted One's concubines that Knee-Capps had been negotiating with, through the harem's ' bush telegraph ', having fancied her,—yashmak and all—through the fine tracery of Moorish screen that separated her from the infidels.

' His ruse, which *nearly* succeeded, was to take a leaf from Cleopatra's book, but instead of having her ladyship secreted in a roll of carpet, stuffed her into the ambassadorial diplomatic pouch. It was a close fit even in that large leather portmanteau, but Lady Mildred made it. Unfortunately, the clasp broke at a vital moment in the journey through the royal quarters, just as the aged Grand Vizier was making his night rounds.

' Heads rolled; needless to say, diplomatic relations with Great Britain were severed too, and a boom was thrown across the Bosphorus. The now infamous infidel, ' Arby ', was re-called, of course (he was quietly transferred to the Cameroons as vice-consul, where he was later eaten by friendly tribes-men). Lady Mildred, who lived to the great age of 103 was always know afterwards (behind her back!) as " the diplo-matic bag "!

' The father, (one of the Bigge-Berkes from Termonfeckin) was prominent in the Land League and had been a friend of Smith O'Brien, but, as a result of bad blood between Cardinal McHale, " The Lion of Tuam ", over the siting of the new Catholic university, and himself (which suggested a slur on the family of Dan O'Connell, " The Liberator ") a feud developed between the families. In an attempt to breach the void, Disraeli offered the Foreshaws the vacant see of Clon-macnoise. Of course, when the Plunkingtons heard this they angrily retorted that they were well capable of appointing their own bishops and required absolutely no assistance from either Downing Street or Saint Peter's.'

At this point our priest, whose index finger had remained stationary on that part of his text that he had been reading since the Pope had launched forth on his, lifted his misty pink eyes over their rimless spectacles, focusing these orbs on a yellowing photograph of the Great Western Hotel in Sligo which, framed behind the papal head, was as near as he could bring himself to looking directly at that disturbingly well-informed party. Even the woman of the west paused in her labour of clearing the condensation from the carriage window —the better to see Rathmogerly—even she forgot her own worries for this once, as these names of the great and holy were flung about her swaying cabin.

' Then there was the brother who was to become the Buddhist monk. He was said to be the love child of the Earl of Dodder and his mother, Lady Rathmogerly, when his Lordship was with the Heavy Brigade in the Crimea. He had survived the charge of Balaclava, having got among the Russian guns at the end of that fatal sally. Indeed, he could display in later years (when master of the Ward Union) the scorch marks, from the gunpowder of the same artillery, on the lace cuffs he had been wearing that day with his hunting pinks.

' It was unfortunate about the uncle', the narrator continued. ' He had been related by marriage to the Fitzroy-Plantagenets and had been a major with the twelfth Lancers serving beside Churchill at the battle of Omdurman in 1898. His wife Nellie (she was famous for her homemade marmalade—hers was a secret recipe, handed down by her family who were themselves, on the spindle side, direct descendants of the last chaplain to Mary, Queen of Scots) became strangely infatuated with James Elroy Flecker to the extent that the major ("Galloping Depravity" as he was known) in a fit of pique, turned his affections to his dogs—ten couples of Basset hounds he kept in his luxurious kennels near George Moore's house in Ely Place.

' There was a tragic outcome and an ensuing scandal so severe that it almost toppled Gladstone's second government when the major was made to stand trial on charges of carnal knowledge of one of the hounds in the back of his landau during the running of the Irish Grand National at Fairyhouse. Despite learned counsel's plea for the defence when it was argued that the dog had not only willingly accepted his master's *amours* but warmly returned them, Lord Chief Justice Baron Palles was moved to give his celebrated ruling that has since become enshrined in the constitution of many lands—*In the case of bestiality, mutual consent is not a good defence. . . .* '

A papal family disquisition, like a Hallowe'en rocket on reaching its final, climactic stage, was permitted to explode as a star, showering the immediate generations with fine ruby clusters of glowing slanders. No point then in pursuing the major's story, which at this peak anyhow branches off into a thousand other anecdotes. Before we had crossed the Shannon at Athlone ' Galloping Depravity ' was buried under an avalanche of the legends of succeeding generations of his seed and breed—who, if anything, were more outlandish than he. But our central nervous system is so constructed as to take just *so* much of the bizarre, and by the time our fiery steed had brought us clamorously into the neighbourhood of Athenry, the reverend father was dozing, mouth open, and we—our Winter's Tale half done—well we were entertaining the westerly woman with a full-blooded fugue based on the Pope's own lusty rendition of the ' Groves of Blarney '.

Where are they now? The contumelious Fitzroys, the arrogant Plantagenets, the Brythons that rode to hounds with the killing Kildares, the Albions who hunted with the Galway Blazers; the hydra-headed Plunkingtons and their odious kinsmen the Foreshaws and *their* wicked uncles? Frankly I don't know.

An unusually tall slender girl with waist length hair the colour of wheat-straw and eyes like two dark green ponds, is smoking pot in a discotheque. She wears a long black gown of faded stuff that might have come out of somebody's attic, a fringed Daniel Boone jacket and mauve boots. Her name has to be Jill and, yes, she is a Plunkington. Her brother Mark is doing 'bird' in the 'Scrubs'. It seems that. . . .

Enough! Who am I to chronicle your saga. The Pope has gone and, like the Queen Maeve, disappeared beyond the sunset. Vanished like the bobbing red tail-light on the Galway Express. Go now your unfabled ways; the Pope's last words are spoken, *Chérie.*

The Pope died quite suddenly in the early spring of 1970. His death came as an entirely unexpected shock and a brutal severance for his myriad friends on two continents. He was a non-drinker (in the Irish sense, permitting himself merely the occasional glass of wine) for the twenty-five years or so during which I had the pleasure of his friendship.

On the other hand, he was very stout. He liked to dine well and his more or less continuous peregrinations took him to many fine mansions and stately homes. His knees, as a consequence, found themselves beneath much groaning mahogany and this may have been a contributory factor in the coronary condition that brought about his death.

Kavanagh admitted to having perpetuated only one Irish 'bull' in his life. Somebody had said that the reason the Pope had so prodigiously developed the art of genealogical anecdotage was that being a poor man he often had to (not to put too fine a tooth on it) 'sing for his supper'. Kavanagh, who unlike myself, thought it all so much humbug, grunted and rejoined: 'He would eat a damn sight better if he kept his mouth shut.'

In the last years of his life he spent much of his time in the United States. Here at last he found a rich and appreciative audience for his talent. His gifts were much in demand both by academics and the public generally. I am told that while he was employed by the University of Southern Illinois as a specialist in its Irish Studies Department, he also ran a sideline in a big supermarket in the local town, Carbondale.

This was nothing less than a booth, somewhere between the deep frozen turkeys and the fresh vegetables, where you could get your lineage and pedigree plus your coat of arms and, of course, a papal disquisition.

A week before he died he dropped a manuscript for me into the Bailey. I had asked him for a contribution for the anthology of Joycean essays I was putting together (*A Bash in the Tunnel*) and this was his essay. All the other contributors had treated with the subject of the author more or less directly. The Pope picked as his theme the real-life Jesuit Father who looms so large in the books. The title was: *Father Conmee and His Associates*. It was so very gossipy and characteristic. . .

Paddy Kavanagh

If ever you go to Dublin town
In a hundred years or so
Inquire for me in Baggot Street
And what I was like to know.—

Patrick Kavanagh : ' If Ever You Go To Dublin Town '

There was a vacuum in literary Dublin after the demise of
Seán O'Faoláin's monthly, *The Bell*. By the middle of 1949 I
was well advanced in my own plans to furnish the city with a
new periodical—this time a non-political magazine of literature and art, which I had tentatively decided to call *Envoy*
(the bearer of a message). What was most needed for this venture was a good ' anchor man ', somebody who could write
well and trenchantly, who could give aim and continuity. My
eye settled on Patrick Kavanagh—but he was unapproachable.
I knew his harsh Monaghan vocabulary too well, had often
heard it pressed into service to repel both friend and foe who
had the hardihood to address him, above all, on literary
matters. I had heard stories—such as the one about the little
American lady with the purple rinse, who asked him had he
ever tried using ' the Alexandrine Hexameter with the internal
atonal rhyme sequence ', to which he, with much asperity,
replied, ' Naaah! But I'll tell you what I did do. I nailed the
liver of a pig against the door of the haggard and — it! '
I might have got off with a simple, ' Axe me arse '—but even
that I was in no mood to relish.

I knew him to see and I knew him by repute. In those days
before discotheques and late-nite drinkeries, you took your girl
friend to the pictures and then gave her a mixed grill in the
balcony restaurant. From much observation I deduced that

Kavanagh was by way of being the Casanova of the cinema cafes. He would have a cheery greeting for my girl friend but not for me. Later, when I was engaged, it was my fiancée to whom he turned his attention, later still her mother. The explanation for his hunting this particular territory was that he was a film critic for the *Standard* at the time. No doubt there were free cups of tea and buns thrown in—as well as the complimentary ticket.

The *Standard* was a weekly Catholic paper. The Irish name, which was printed under the masthead, was ' An tIoláir ' (Paddy called it ' The Tiller '). He worked in all departments, even writing leaders and hagiography as the occasion demanded. The leader-writers had instructions from the top not to repeat the word ' Pope ' monotonously in their deathless prose. They were advised to vary it. As he put the matter himself in an excerpt from his ' Diary ' in *Envoy*—itself supposedly a précis of a review of Anthony Cronin's biography, *He Was God* (a work pertaining to himself, Kavanagh)—which would be published in the *Weekly Irish Herald Tribune* (incorporating the *Irish Times*) for 1 May 2021 A.D. :

> He took on a job on a pious paper and wrote, week after week, stories about people who were ' defaming the name of our beloved Cardinal.' So eager was he to succeed as a sycophant in the pious line that he had nine names for the Pope—The Pope, Holy Father, His Holiness, Supreme Pontiff, Vicar of Christ, Visible Head of the Church, Angelic Shepherd, Successor of Saint Peter, Bishop of Rome—and the rest, which he could only remember occasionally.

John Henry, Cardinal McRory, was Archbishop of Armagh and Primate of All Ireland. His life was drawing to a close. Ireland prayed. The staff of the ' Tiller ' kept all-night vigil—the reverential silence scarcely disturbed by the swish of obituary-composing quills. The front page was being held open for the editor's final headline and lead-in paragraph. A phone rang. Somebody lifted the receiver and listened. There was complete silence in the office as he slowly replaced the instrument. ' His

Grace ', he sighed, ' has just passed away.' ' Now he knows what I always knew ', broke in Paddy. ' What's that then?' enquired the editor. ' There's no God!' answered Paddy. Dublin was not long in hearing about that one and for years afterwards it was the cause of many a guilty chuckle.

He had been a friend of John Betjeman when the latter was press attaché at the United Kingdom embassy in Dublin during the war years. It had been said that Betjeman had hoped to entice Kavanagh into the British secret service and to that end even proposed that Kavanagh should learn Portuguese before insinuating himself as an Axis sympathizer into Nazi circles in Lisbon. Alas for comic history—Paddy, in the role of Inniskeen's answer to James Bond, prowling the Tagus, plague of the Hitlerian war machine—remains an intriguing possibility. Betjeman drove a car—as a member of the diplomatic corps he was one of the élite that had the privilege during the Emergency. In a poem ' I Had A Future ', there occur the lines:

> *Show me the stretcher-bed I slept on*
> *In a room on Drumcondra Road,*
> *Let John Betjeman call for me in a car.*

The dispatches of his diplomatic friend were only released from their secret classification by the Public Records Office in London in 1972 after the already beKnighted poet had received the Laureateship. They make interesting reading. One of his tasks was to persuade the Irish people that Nazi Germany was persecuting the Catholics. He believed that the *Universe* newspaper and the now defunct *Picture Post* were his best methods of persuasion.

The following résumé is taken from the *Irish Times* of November 1972:

In a report to the director of the Catholic section of the Ministry of Information on March 14th, 1941, Sir John said: ' I find even among the most sincere Catholics a refusal to believe in stories of German persecution.'

Sir John said that Catholics with German sympathies—and he

named an *Irish Independent* columnist—always said that these stories were British propaganda. He claimed that the biggest Catholic newspaper, *The Standard,* was ' most tendentious and difficult. Its chief lines are that the Catholics in the North are persecuted—which is true and a sure sales-getter—and that the war is one of big business.'

The *Standard,* he claimed, maintained that of the two ' belligerents ' Germany had less big business than Britain because she did more for the unemployed and therefore it would be better if Germany won.

He said that he had made great friends with the editor (Peadar Curry), and was trying to show him that Germany was anti-Christian.

Sir John asked London to get the editor of *The Universe,* an English Catholic newspaper, roughly equivalent to *The Standard,* to publish straightforward illustrated articles of the persecution of Polish Catholics by the Nazis.

From these dispatches and the importance HM Government attached to the role of the *Standard* in the propaganda war, it is possible to surmise that the future Laureate's friendship for Kavanagh was not quite as altruistic as it seemed at the time to be.

Long after the war, on a visit to London, Paddy called on Betjeman who was then literary editor of *Time and Tide.* Betjeman was either too busy to see him, or if he did, was too abrupt or in some way slighted him. In the next printing of the poem it is *John Ryan* who is calling for him in the car! Truth to tell, I was only able to manage a bicycle in those days and even that was mostly stabled in the bicycle shed down in Clongowes.

One day I was walking along Grafton Street with Sean O'Sullivan when I observed Paddy approaching us on a collision course. ' Now,' I urged him, ' stop him and introduce us.' Sean knew him well, being one of his cronies in the Palace Bar (in those days, at its apogee as poetasters' pub). He was a bigger all-round man than Paddy so he was able to block him, though the scowl on Paddy's face made it clear that he was in no mood to be stopped by anybody. During the introduction he groaned piteously. With not a little trepidation, I broached the subject of *Envoy*, asking him would he care to contribute a poem or something. He looked at me in utter loathing, let out a dying roar, and took off down the street under full rig. O'Sullivan, who (as it happened) liked me, gave chase and in his own equally intimidating voice demanded why the so-and-so he couldn't have the civility to answer (me) his friend. Paddy at last relented and it was agreed that we go into the nearest pub. Over some large whiskies he consented to write a ' diary ' for the magazine, a promise which he faithfully kept for the whole two years of *Envoy's* existence. It was the beginning of a friendship that was to last for the rest of his life—twenty turbulent years.

I began to meet him regularly, mainly in McDaid's which I had used since the old war days when MacNamara and I had studios in Grafton Street. His routine then was to get up at dawn (the country customs die hard) and write until the shops opened. Back then with the newspapers to study form. Write for another hour or so, then debauch into Baggotonia generally. A visit to Parson's bookshop, a talk with the children in the sad courts of Pembroke Road, perhaps a drink or two in the Waterloo lounge, Searsons or Mooneys, then tram to Dawson Street, thence by foot to Graftonia and, ultimately, McDaid's. Further drinks would be consumed while young acolytes of the poetic muse would be peppered with broadsides of abuse.

Around about mid-day, Irish or English racing would commence. One would be forgiven for thinking that this marked the serious beginning of the working day, such was the energy with which he and all the other Grafton Street punters threw themselves into the fray. Twenty years before Britain had book-makers' shops, Dublin had them (there were about a dozen within easy reach of McDaid's). The punters would work on the picking of their nags and return to the pubs at fifteen-minute intervals.

J. P. Donleavy, in his introduction to *The Ginger Man*,

recalls ' early morning poets talking their earnest way to the better betting shops, making a conversational exchange with the clerk to ask what's a good thing today. Then the morning's tension 'till the crazy afternoon when the nags are let loose and the poets pray . . . . '

I remember once being with Kavanagh and company in convivial Neary's (of Chatham Street) when we were joined by the important English poet, John Heath-Stubbs. After the consumption of a number of pints someone announced that there was a novice's hurdle at Market Rasen that needed his immediate attention. Heath-Stubbs, who was partly blind, tagged on behind us as we made our progress to the betting offices of Joseph and Maurice Mirrelson in Anne Street. Never having even seen a bookie's shop, but dimly apprehending a counter, assistants and noisy, beery customers, Heath-Stubbs, thinking that we were in yet another bar, called for a fresh round for the whole company.

The afternoon would eventually diffuse in a haze of alcohol and gambling fever, depending on how successful their horses were in the outcome of the many engagements of the day. There would be seven different meetings with six races to a meeting with, say, twenty horses in each race—over eight hundred probable starters, with all the permutations and combinations inherent therein. During the period of the English flat-racing season (April-November) something like 6,000 horses run in 2,625 races over 37 flat race-courses scattered from Hamilton to Brighton, and from Yarmouth to Liverpool. The immense scope of this operation is taken on gratefully by the Irish punter in addition to what he takes to be his local gambling duties. Night would fall and Paddy would come home, circuitously, to Pembroke Road to recharge the batteries for the following day.

In your equine heaven, do you know what hours, days, years, versifiers spent in your service to the neglect of poetry and health, O Prince Regent, Caughoo, Sheila's Cottage, Hatton's Grace, Early Mist, Devon Loch, Quare Times, Papa Fourway, E.S.B., Hardy Canute, Nicholas Silver, Arkle?

He had one long lucky spell that baffled bookmaker and fellow-punter alike. He began to make astonishing sums of money by backing horses that had no form yet consistently won. One bookmaker thought that he had top-secret inside information from the stables and simply refused to take any more bets from him. In fact, all that he had been doing was to back horses with the letter 'Z' in their names, regardless of their owner, jockey, pedigree or price.

But back to that first meeting in Grafton Street; it took place (as though destiny had arranged it) at one of the crucial turning points of his life when he was reaching the end of his 'pastoral' period. Ten years hacking in Dublin, ten awful years of writing film reviews and leaders for a religious newspaper had, it seemed, emptied the last of his poetic reserves. It was impossible to draw further from the bank of his rustic youth. *Envoy*, luckily, was there at the precise time when he was about to propound something altogether new. It was a critical time in his development, comparable with his later, pivotal moment by the banks of the Grand Canal in the summer of 1955, when he realized that his 'purpose was to have no purpose.'

What he achieved in the span of *Envoy's* life was to be the most sustained, confident and lucid period of creative writing of his career. Indeed, when the magazine finally 'folded' such was the momentum that had carried him, he simply *had* to replace it with something else and that something else became *Kavanagh's Weekly*.

But to return to earlier days; shortly after our first encounter we met again, this time in a coffee house. He was still a bit of a 'bun man' (as he used to call Frank O'Connor and Yeats) at that time, and was only beginning to develop into a seriously committed drinker. He was talking of pretentiousness in men, particularly among men of letters; writers who covet awards and distinctions, those that would leave you 'just for a riband to wear in their coats.' He put it this way; the Sioux warrior dressed for battle in a head-dress of feathers, from the crown of

H

the head to the ground, but they were *turkey* teathers; the
chief of the tribe wore only a single feather. It was the feather
of the high-flying eagle. In all the misfortunes and hard times
that clung to him, no matter how decrepit and battered he
became, I always mentally saw him wearing that single,
defiant, feather.

The stuff of comedy was always lying about Kavanagh's
path. He was usually the first to be tripped by it. He was
living in Pembroke Road at the time. I called to see him one
day in his bed-sit, in a tall, late-Georgian building, to collect
further material, but really to get him to correct proofs, a
task for which he had little or no appetite. I believe he liked
this flat more than any of the other apartments he lived in
during his thirty peripatetic Dublin years. I remember the
bathroom on the left as one went in. The bath itself bore sad
testimony to Paddy's wifeless existence, being full to the brim
with empty sardine and soup tins. The main room was a
desolation—ankle-deep in papers and typescript. Somewhere
in the middle was a table with a typewriter. The window
had the driver's rear mirror from a truck attached to it—this
was used for studying callers at the hall-door, without their
knowing.

Once upon a time strolling down Grafton Street, he looked
into the window of a large new English furniture store that
had lately and optimistically opened its doors to the discern-
ing Dublin public. Fantastic inducements to the shoppers
were being offered. Paddy saw a hideous Chesterfield suite
with a sign saying, 'Absolutely No Deposit—10/- a month.
Easy Payments!' On an impulse he entered the store, ordered
the suite, pausing only to include a huge radiogram in the
deal as well. That evening a pantechnicon arrived, depositing
the furniture. It was an uncommonly simple and economical
method of furnishing a flat, providing, like him you con-
temptuously dismissed the whole bit about the repayments,
easy or not.

True, they did call on him one day on foot of a court order
to repossess but Paddy, spotting them in the handy rear-mirror,

offered to return it there and then by dropping it out of the window. I don't think anything more was heard about the matter. It was still there when I used to visit.

Come to think of it, he must have got a carpet thrown in too. . . . I recall the problem he had in disposing of the old one, a verminous article, saturated in stale stout and riddled with cigarette burns. Eventually he had to cut it into small strips and smuggle it out at night under his coat. Residents of Waterloo, Wellington and Clyde Roads were surprised in the morning to find rotting Axminster amongst their lobelias or peering from behind their virginia creeper.

The bathtub, full of rusty sardine tins, reminds me that his principal culinary tool was a tin-opener. Notwithstanding, he once had a princely meal there. He was walking up to Tommy Ryan's in Haddington Road, when he saw a mallard, or common wild duck (most likely strayed from the pond in St Stephen's Green) caught on the spiked railings along by the canal. Paddy went to recover it. Possibly his original intentions were good, but the primitive hunter must have come out in him (memories of poaching salmon in the river Fane, as a boy, probably crowded his brain), for instead of bringing it to the Cats' and Dogs' Home (as he had promised several solicitous old ladies who had assembled— out of nowhere) he nipped smartly back to Pembroke Road, wrung the duck's neck, plucked, cleaned, roasted and ate it. ' It melted in me mouth like butter ', he confided in me later.

Another time I found him in bed, badly shaken, with what appeared to be a rash, but was in reality a mass of cuts and abrasions to face and hands. He was breathing heavily. I asked him what had happened. ' Oh dear,' he began and then proceeded to fill me in. It was, he related, his habit, when he had washed his socks, to hang them out on the window-sill to dry. A gust of wind the previous night had caught them and blown them off—and into the back garden below. He had encountered this dilemma before and to that end always retained a handy length of stout rope, for the lady who rented the basement flat (he having fallen foul of her,

for one reason or another) refused to allow him to go through
her apartment—the only orthodox means of entering the
garden. He had, he repeated, this rope and would shinny
down it, collect the lost article, climb out over the back wall
and re-enter the house by the front door, thence up to the flat,
there to regain the rope. His anchor or bollard for the rope
was the gas-meter affixed to the wall. This particular morning,
looking at the meter, a doubt arose in his mind concerning its
ability to take much more of the sort of stresses it was having
to sustain, however well, indeed nobly, it had rendered its
service in the past.

Clearly something more sturdy was now required. A very
large iron and brass fender, weighing about two hundred-
weight, surrounded the fire place. It was a great deal wider
than the window, so that if it did, for any reason, move, it
could not, he argued, physically come through. To this he
might have added ' *longways* that is ' because when he came
to make his descent and was halfway down the wall, the
fender began to move, the slip-knot slipped to one of the
extremes, allowing thereby the fender, now all set to join
Paddy in his plunge, to emerge, which it duly did. Both then
hurtled through the roof of the bicycle shed beneath and, in
furtherance of Galileo's theory, simultaneously. It was a spectacular affair by all accounts and Martin Kelly, who was sleeping in another flat in the same house, told me that he thought
a light aircraft had crashed into the building.

It was in the telling of such stories, with a grim and
hilarious panache, that made him the good companion he was.
Another time he told how, in lean days, he worked as a can-
vasser for a mutual friend. Our friend's business was that of
journeymen spray painters. They travelled up and down the
country spray-painting barns and cowsheds and kindred agri-
cultural out-offices, with portable spray-painting apparatus.
Kavanagh's job was to go ahead and secure the orders. Big
houses were a natural target; the owner could afford to have
the work done and would possess the necessary number of out-

buildings to make a stop worthwhile. One day he discovered, at the end of a mile long avenue, with a file of immense cedars on either side, a mansion of heroic dimensions, in full-blooded Palladian style. One of the stately homes of Ireland, to be sure. Here, if anywhere, would be found spray-painting possibilities worthy of a man (he reflected) as he got his first glimpse of the superb barns, cider presses, grain-silos, stables and cowsheds that stood at a respectful distance from the baronial hall. Eagerly he crossed the moat and mounted the granite steps, making his way past the ceramic tigers captured at the siege of Peking. I cannot disclose the name of the owners of the house, but in order to do justice to the story I shall ask to be allowed to call them simply, Sir Harry and Lady Winifred Orme-Pitt.

With some apprehension, Paddy pulled the doorbell. In the lower bowels of the mansion a brazen tongue clanged its answer. Some time passed before the butler opened the oaken door. Handing in his card he asked to see the owner or the head steward. The butler ordered him to wait. . . . Presently a lady in Donegal tweeds and wellingtons appeared. It was the Lady Winifred. Without further ado, Paddy launched into his spiel. He explained fluently the advantages to be gained and the rewards to be achieved by having their property painted. His was a new and greatly improved painting method, and was being offered at so keen a price only because the company was in the locality at the time and costs could accordingly be trimmed. What matter if some of the red oxide did settle on the hay? It contained invaluable iron which, in small quantities, was actually beneficial to cows! She was a frail little lady who listened with a genteel smile as Paddy continued his sales talk. His overtures finished, Lady Winifred told him she would have to see Sir Harry himself and disappeared into the gloomy, cavernous interior.

Presently, angry noises, obviously the output of Sir Harry, filled the house from which Paddy could distinguish whole words like ' Tell . . . bloody fellow . . . not off . . . lands . . .

five minutes . . . get . . . gamekeepers . . . fire on him . . .'
Hounds straining on leashes, in doggy unison, growled alarm-
ingly. Curses, expletives and whines shattered what was left of
his composure as Lady Winifred emerged, ashen-faced, from
the inner cavity. The sadly polite smile still lingered on her
mouth; ' Frightfully sorry ', she murmured, ' but I'm afraid its
a lemon . . . !'

Another time, to make ends meet, he took on a job
' travelling ' for a patent fire-grate manufacturer. I try to
think of him in the typical setting of the commercial room
of a seedy provincial hotel, surrounded by men ' in light
stationery ' and kindred artifacts, swapping old, dirty stories
—but my mind wobbles too much. The climax of this
particular career arrived when the hardware buyer of a big
department store was deprecating the grate—probably to get
the price down a bit. It was no more than the time-honoured
ploy of the reluctant buyer requiring in return the statutory
' hard sell '. To his amazement, Paddy fully agreed with him,
putting an end to the loathsome business by saying, ' not only
is it ridiculously expensive, but it's also a total load of bloody
rubbish.' With that he stormed out leaving the discredited
sample, as heavy and as awkward as a bag of coal, for the
buyer to sort out at his leisure.

A venture more to his taste, the object of which was also
to beat the ' economic rap ', was his newspaper, *Kavanagh's
Weekly*. Years later when we were talking about our respec-
tive publications, one of the things discussed was the problem
of disposing of returned copies. In my case, the weight and
bulk of these unwanted copies of *Envoy* constituted a major
headache, though I finally wheedled the Red Cross into
taking much of it. When it came to P.K.'s turn, and of
course, he had a worse problem, the Red Cross were no longer
accepting paper for pulping. The Corporation dustmen did
not accept inflammable matter for disposal either, so that was
the dustbin out. You could hire a lorry to go out to the big
tip at Ringsend and get rid of it there—but that cost money
—so the answer was to *burn*. Soon the flat in Pembroke Road

came to resemble the stokehold of the *Ile de France,* as Paddy and brother Peter, stripped to the waist, fed a seemingly-inexhaustible supply of returned *Weeklies* to the fireplace. Though heat and smoke were intolerable stoke they must, though bale followed bale, as the newspaper remorselessly continued to arrive at the door. The conflagration continued for many a week. Mighty plumes of black smoke ascended during the day while by night the Pembroke skyline was an orange glow; like a mediaeval lighthouse or Pharo it proclaimed its presence by smoke during the day and naked flame by night.

I worked with him on the early issues of the *Weekly.* In fact, I have the distinction of having drawn, with my own hand, the ' banner ' or masthead of the journal. I also did the theatre and radio notes. These were respectively entitled, ' The Mummers ' and ' The Wireless '—on the editor's orders. As contributors were not paid, he ended up by writing the entire paper, including the letters-to-the-editor, himself.

At that time the big circulation papers like the *Sunday Press* and the *Sunday Independent* were offering motor cars as prizes in their weekly fashion competitions. The competition, obligingly contrived to impose the least tax on the most pea-sized of brains, was to select from a bevy of vapid bathing beauties the one which, in the reader's opinion, was the least awful, and the rest according to choice. As the permutations on this numbers game were so vast, your chances of winning were about as remote as that of winning the Irish Hospitals Sweep. The car would eventually be handed to the lucky somebody on the stage of the Theatre Royal, Dublin's huge ' palace of varieties '.

Paddy, not to be outdone, also ran a competition. He apologized to his readers for being unable, due to costs, to publish the actual photographs of his bathing belles—instead, the readers were asked to content themselves with the capital letter that appeared under the picture of each beauty. The prize offered was a model T Ford which would be presented on the stage of the Abbey Theatre. It almost goes without saying that the winning combination of letters read C**T.

When the paper folded, Paddy said goodbye to what was left of his youth and his dreams. There were great things yet to come from him but his confidence in his financial future as a writer was gone for good.

He had a contract with the publishers Macmillan, which gave him a modest weekly allowance in return for the complete rights to publish all his work. He had completed the novel *Tarry Flynn*, but the devil in the guise of another publisher offered a fairly large cash payment which he was unable to refuse. The novel was duly published, the publisher went bankrupt, he was never paid and Macmillans tore up the contract.

Money, or the want of it, was the problem of every day, while writing—merely to make it—became life's most detestable grind. If he could have found yet another way to beat the rap he would, but he was by now virtually unemployable. I remember he applied for the post of curator of the Municipal Gallery of Modern Art, but I'm afraid that was another lemon.

Once in the fish bar of the old Bailey, I was having a meal with Ole Sarvig, the distinguished Danish poet who was visiting Ireland at the time, when Paddy walked in. When Ole realized who he was he begged me to introduce them— which I did with some trepidation. There ensued this dialogue:

> Me: May I introduce Ole Sarvig, the distinguished . . .
> P.K.: Whaaa?
> Ole: I am being Ole Sarvig, Danish poet and . . .
> P.K.: You dirty—!
> Ole: (much distressed) Why for you call me such a horrible thing?
> P.K.: You killed our last Árd Rí!

For the uninformed the Árd Rí was the high king of ancient

Ireland. The personage whom Paddy had in mind was Brian Ború who was killed by the Danes, while saying his prayers in a tent during the Battle of Clontarf (Dublin), in the year A.D. 1014. The Irish have long, though not invariably accurate, memories—the last Árd Rí was Ruaidhrí Ó Conchubhair (Rory O'Connor) who set up his royal capital in Tuam in the year 1164, just five years before the Anglo-Norman invasion.

A further poetic confrontation took place at a time when we were both visiting the English metropolis in the early 'fifties. This time it was with the celebrated Welsh poet, Dylan Thomas. Kitty Epstein, the sculptor's daughter, who at that time was married to Lucien Freud, the painter, invited us to a pub in Chelsea to meet the great man. Paddy, who was genuinely respectful in front of professionals whom he admired, shook hands warmly, murmuring a most un-Kavanagh-like piece of politeness to the effect that it was a great pleasure to make his acquaintance. Thomas was sitting at a small circular table on which stood the remnants of about fourteen pints of bitter. I remember thinking it strange that he should be swilling beer when all the odds were that he should have graduated to smatháns of malt by this stage. It was about a year before his death.

The Thomasian answer to the Kavanagh cordiality was to insult him by putting on a dreadful stage-Irish accent, the sort a very poor English vaudeville performer might try on the second house on a Saturday night in Bradford:

Yerra, begorra, and sure if it isn't the bould Paddy Kavanagh his sel' that's after wandering over from the four fair green fields of the ould sod itself, the craythur, alanna mo croi, intoirely . . .

Paddy pretended to ignore this daft dialogue but I could tell that he was deeply hurt by it. A great silence descended upon him so, to fill the gap at it were, I leaned across the sea of froth and asked Thomas straight out if he would give me a poem for *Envoy*.

' Yes,' he replied (reverting to his BBC Third voice), ' if you pay me the same as the *Ladies Home Journal*. Fifty pounds a poem.'

That was about the equivalent of two hundred and fifty pounds in present-day money. Shortly afterwards we left; Kitty very nearly in tears (she had been ignored though she had given a dinner for Thomas the night before). Paddy was in his huff but I was happily indifferent, being young in the big city, and chuckled inwardly at this encounter of the two poets. It is sad now to think that it was their only meeting.

He often told me of early attempts at versifying—in his salad days when he was at the crossroads, with the choice of being a poet or a farmer. A local provincial paper announced (with suitable flourishes) a Grand Poetry Competition. The first prize was to be five shillings, the second two-and-sixpence, and the third a book-token for a shilling. The subject was to be anything beautiful one had seen in the countryside.

The prospect of substantial money dangled before him encouraged Paddy to work hard and long on a pastoral theme —after all, he felt this was *his* line of country. His great expectations were not wholly dashed when the paper duly gave the results and his poem, over which he had toiled so long, won the second prize. But what really did infuriate him was the fact that the winner had sent in Joyce Kilmer's *Trees*—under his own name—Maolseachlain O'Toole, of Crossmaglen!

The memory of this trick-of-the-loop man and his poem brazenly beginning with ' I think that I shall never see . . .' all over the front page of the *Clones Argus* (or was it the *Newry Newsletter*?) complete with his picture would bring a chuckle from Paddy forty years later. His reminiscence would usually be wound up with the pithy and proven couplet:

From Carrickmacross to Crossmaglen
You'll meet more rogues than honest men.

An ecclesiastical generalissimo (noted for his administrative adroitness and glacial stillness), Most Rev. Dr. John Charles McQuaid, the late Roman Catholic Archbishop of Dublin, once called upon Paddy, bearing gifts! It was during the Pembroke Road years in the season of Advent. The apartment, as has been remarked, was noted neither for its tidiness nor its cleanliness. But on this occasion, quite apart from the matter of ecclesiastical hygiene, Paddy was heavily involved in the business of entertaining a young lady of uncertain virtue. A very dodgy business in the fair city.

A sharp knock at the door brought Paddy to his radar screen. He quickly digested the information contained in its concave mirror, viz: Archbishop's chauffeur-driven Austin Princess; Archbishop's secretary, Monsignor   , at the door, knocking. Hurriedly adjusting his dress, he took a series of lemming-like plunges down the stairs and opened the door —on the chain.

'Goodnight, Father. What brings ye to a place like this . . . ? '

' His Grace has asked me to convey the compliments of the season. May he come in? '

' Ah God, Father, I couldn't ask him in—the flat is in a terrible condition. It's no fit place for a man of his eminence. Look, there's people living here you wouldn't find in the Gloucester Diamond . . .'

' The Archbishop is fully cognisant of your circumstances, Mr Kavanagh, and far from taking offence at what is, after all, the holy condition of poverty, and mindful of our Saviour whose birth we commemorate at this time of the year, a birth, let us say without any irreverence, which was characterized by the absence of even the rudiments of comfort, nay . . .'

' But the place is a total dread—the man who was to come to fix the jacks, the lavatory, today—oh you couldn't have *him* in this squalid tenement, Father, you couldn't . . .'

' Believe me, His Grace would account it a peculiar favour . . .'

Paddy, by dint of desperation, prevailed. The Monsignor

stepped down to the shining sedan. Returning, he said that His Grace understood and would he, Mr Kavanagh, care to join him in the car? This was done with alacrity and pleasure. In time Paddy emerged laden with presents of a handknitted sweater, a bottle of Powers Gold Label and 200 Sweet Afton. Finally, when benedictions and salutations were being exchanged through the car door, his ear caught the alarming sound of his own window being raspingly flung open above. He now had to roar his farewells for fear that any commentary directed at him from the flat might reach the Archbishop's ears. To the accompaniment of these noises, he fairly pushed the Austin down Pembroke Road and into the merciful oblivion of the night.

He liked talking, particularly to himself and quite loudly too. Another poet I knew spoke softly to the shade of Sarah Bernhardt, but Paddy spoke brusquely and noisily to himself. It was a characteristic he had inherited from his father.

One day I was attempting to describe the intensity of the colour black in a certain context. He or it, I claimed, was ' as black as the riding boots of the Earl of Hell.' It was a description an old shellback had once given me, one of his many remarkable similes, an accumulation of which studded his speech like barnacles the hull of a Cape-Horner. Paddy chewed over what I said and liked it.

' As black as the riding boots of the Err-ill of Hell—be the hokey-fly, damn me sowl, that's a good wan . . .', he murmured happily.

Later in the day, snatching at a handy interval between the closing of the pubs and the first race at Doncaster, he entered an eating-house (or cafe) called the Horseshoe in Upper Baggot Street to partake of a bite of lunch. His mind was far away, mostly in Doncaster no doubt, but a part of it still toyed with ʾhat earlier remark of mine.

' *As black* . . . (he stuffed a large boiled potato covered with

H.P. sauce into his mouth and masticated studiously awhile) *as the bloody riding boots* . . . (he lifted a chop, held it in front of him for a moment before his huge ivory-tinted molars clamped on it like a monstrous gin-trap) *of the Err-ill of Hell*!'

Then, for the first time, he noticed his companion across the table. He was a young house surgeon from the nearby Royal City of Dublin Hospital. Paddy saw him through his misty spectacles as through a glass darkly. He looked bewildered, even on the verge of tears. He was a Nubian—from the Sudan. He was so black that it could not be described as a pigment at all—for it was beyond colour; it was the blackness of the interior of a coalmine on a starless, moonless night. It was the nadir of darkness. Paddy mumbled some kind of apology and fled.

Kavanagh had been an athlete in his young days, playing football for Inniskeen, doing the high-jump, the long-jump and pulling in the local tug-of-war team. One Sunday, Peter, Paddy, Patrick Swift and I made the journey to the Widow Flavin's pub in Sandyford (it must have been too fine a day to drink in town). One of the big Gaelic inter-provincial matches was being played in Croke Park. In Ireland, the entire nation talks or thinks of nothing else when these games are in progress.

The radio must have broken down in the Widow's for no sooner were we well in than a young fellow, somewhat the worse for drink, asked,

' Who's winnin ', mister?'

Paddy affected not to know what he was talking about. He then enacted the role of a man being illuminated by the dawn of understanding.

' Ah, the big match? Well, before stumps was drawn Australia was sixty-five for four in the first innings. . . .'

' Oh, you're very funny, mister ', said the bowsy spitting emphatically between our feet before rejoining his comrades, as dismal a confederation of motiveless bully-boys as one could hope to see.

However we thought no more of the matter, but spent an enjoyable hour or so quaffing pints and exchanging stories. Sooner than we realized, it was the closing hour and the barmen were calling ' Time '. It behoved us now to file out from our cosy gloom into the bright guilt-laden summer afternoon. Peter Kavanagh was first out. Our friend of the earlier encounter, with about six others, was waiting. He approached Peter with his hand out.

' No hard feeling, mister? ' he queried, as with his other arm he attempted a left side-swipe at his head.

Peter, who had boxed for Dublin University, had read this telegraph and knew it was coming, dodged and deftly responded with a leaden fist square on the jaw. With that the whole scene exploded. We were all involved in a stupendous punch-up. I quite literally *threw* one of the gang to the ground, so agitated did I become by the unexpectedness of the affair, because I remember the sound as his head hit the curb.

Paddy waded in warmly with his size twelve Monaghan boots while the brother sent all comers scattering with meticulously placed punches. The mêlée lasted for perhaps five minutes. The very last of the action was when all of the gang, save two, were laid low and these two were grappling with me. The first had his hands around my throat. We were all weak by this stage and I saw Paddy rolling past like a sailor at the end of his shore leave.

' Paddy ', I roared, to attract attention to my plight.

He saw and immediately appraised the situation. Without hesitation, he took a running kick at the outside assailant, as though he was taking a penalty before the goal for the Grattan's (his old team), landing a kick of cup-winning ferocity in your man's derrière. He must have connected with the anal bone, because there was a dull but reassuring dry click. In his spasm, the first garrotter keeled over backwards quite rigidly, dragging his mate (now irreversibly attached by paralysed arms) with him. I somehow managed to avoid becoming the apex of this human pyramid—but at the expense of collar and tie, both of which adornments were ripped off, as Paddy remarked later, ' clean and clever '.

Their losses were total. All had been knocked out. Paddy had lost his spectacles; I had, in addition, my trousers torn from the pocket to the turn-ups; but that was all. We got into the car speedily and zoomed out of Sandyford.

When Paddy returned from the first of what were to be many visits to New York (Peter, the brother, lives there) he was full of all sorts of old Yankee saws and modern instances. One expression that seemed to have greatly grabbed him was ' Scotch on the rocks! ' We were in the old Waterloo Lounge one day and he called out this order to a dubious barman at the other end of the room. He was clearly uncomfortable and finally felt obliged to seek advice from a higher authority. After some furtive whispered exchange with the foreman the curate returned, his hands turned out in sad refusal.

' I'm sorry, Mr Kavanagh,' he says, ' we can't give anyone credit.'

In the *Caves de France* pub in Soho (because of the relative smallness of the English as against the Irish measure) he liked to call for ' two Scotch on the rocks—in the same glass.'

Paddy was no name-dropper—if a name meant anything to him he liked to hold onto it, and possibly caress it. He would sometimes recall his early publisher, Harold Macmillan, later to become Prime Minister, though he had sometimes heard the chimes at midnight with his son, Maurice. He liked to tell us about a Bacchanalia they both shared in Dublin's sober and priest-haunted Gresham Hotel —but that, as they say, was another story. He would refer from time to time to his patron and friend, the Earl of Iveagh, the head of the Guinness clan, in tones verging on true reverence. In his last years he had served as a judge on the panel of the Guinness Poetry Award, an appointment which *inter alia* permitted him to stay free in distinguished London

hotels (like Browns) and be able to have roast chickens and
bottles of Scotch sent to his bedroom by room-service.

But the name which could stop the chatter was that of
Maxim Litvinov. Litvinov was the first People's Commissar
for Foreign Affairs of the new-born Soviet Union, and later
its first Ambassador to the United States. During the years
in the wilderness, when the other Bolshevik founding fathers
were hatching plots or, like Lenin, scheming in the same
Zurich cafe as James Joyce chose to relax from the labours of
Ulysses, Litvinov was a door-to-door pedlar in Ireland. (It
has been said that his mother was Irish—which may explain
his geographic preference.) Paddy remembered well his
occasional visits to the humble Kavanagh dwelling in
Mucker and how Mr Litvinov would come in the door, open
his carpet-bag and lay out on the kitchen table his spread of
alarm clocks, holy pictures, combs, costume jewellery, toys,
and other exotic trinkets. As the gentlemen of the commercial travellers' fraternity would say, he was in ' haber-
dashery ' in Cavan and Monaghan when the poet was a boy
—a long time, an aeon, before a certain sealed train rattled
into the Finland Station in Moscow to the wonder of a world
grown suddenly tremulous. The name Litvinov returned to
prominence when his grandson, Pavel, not long after
Kavanagh's death, was sentenced to five years' exile for his
part in the protest in Red Square against the Russian invasion
of Czechoslovakia.

Paddy, too, had his Great Trial which took place in 1954.
The transcript of this awesome lawsuit may be read in
Kavanagh's own *Collected Pruse.* The issue at stake was an
article printed in the *Leader*—a so-called profile of the poet
which, he claimed, held him up to odium, ridicule and contempt, and to be a libel. Reading it again, it has to be allowed
that it was a reasonably fair (if uncharitable) description of
the man, as he then was, holding court in McDaid's in Harry
Street. What was clear, even then, was that in taking this
action he was about to embark on the most disastrous voyage
of his life. If youth had expired with *Kavanagh's Weekly,*

old age would set in before this trial finally ended. I was
called in, with others, as a character witness. One of these
was Dr Thomas Bodkin, keeper of the Barber Institute in
Birmingham and the author of a work attacking contemporary art. There was a mutual loathing between us, though we
sat side by side for nearly two weeks. As it turned out, we
were never called to give evidence. The defence claimed that
it had never questioned the plaintiff's character. Day followed
tedious day of crafty innuendo, turgid repartee, the fiction of
ignorance and all the dull grey verbal savagery of the law. So
many parties were enjoined in the action—printer, publisher,
distributor, solicitors holding watching briefs, senior counsels,
junior counsels, bewigged snoopers from other courts, that the
whole scene resembled nothing so much as a flight of scald-
crows descending on a potato field. For indeed, did not these
bewigged attorneys, eyes alight with the prospect of the rich
pickings that this sort of lawsuit must inevitably yield,
resemble the crows of Shancoduff as they scanned the fields of
ripening kale in Mucker and Rocksavage, long ago?

I was familiar enough with litigation to realize that the
costs were going to be enormous; and they were. At some
stage of the trial Brendan Behan, who felt that he must,
somehow, get in on the act, approached me to ask if Paddy
would allow him to give evidence on his behalf. This offer
was rejected with a great show of feeling, but the net result
of the snub was that Brendan succeeded in getting evidence
introduced for the defence, which turned the whole case
against the plaintiff.

Kavanagh had denied, in cross-examination, knowing
Behan, but the defence lawyer (John A. Costello, SC, one
time Premier of the Irish Free State) was able to produce, in
evidence, a book the title page of which was inscribed: ' To
my friend Behan, poet and painter—from Patrick Kavanagh.'
When I heard this, I remembered well the occasion when
Paddy got Brendan to paint his flat (he finished the ceiling in
a tomato red, as I recall) and Paddy had given him this book. I
knew the impression this was making on the jury (a group of

I

men whose sympathies would lie closer to the proletarian Brendan than the arrogant Patrick) was far from good, but, in fact, it was disastrous.

He was contumelious enough by any standards but this arrogance was such that mean folk, or those who *believed* that they themselves belonged to a lower class, saw in him a member of some remote caste (one to which, say, politicians might conceivably belong) fallen on evil days, no doubt, but yet privileged in a way that they could never be. One of the few compensations he got during the latter years was in continuously making this distinction clear. In fact, he was poorer and more neglected than most. On his first visit as a young man to Dublin, when he walked for three days from Inniskeen, crossing, as he was later to remark, the lands of only three men to make the journey from his native heath to the outskirts of Dublin, he stayed at the Iveagh Hostel for men. This is a night shelter run on much the same lines as the Salvation Army hostels, which Brendan Behan would have known so well, but Paddy took it to be a hotel and a damned good one at that. Did it not, glory be! have sheets on the beds, the convenience of the modern invention of the electric light and—wonders!—indoor toilets? A bit pricey maybe—a shilling a night—but then, good God, everything had gone up since the war and wasn't the price of cigarettes that much for twenty, and Guinness (who built the hostel) charging half that for a pint? Don't be talking . . .

The libel action was the most forlorn of lost causes. A fund was raised for the appeal. Many people supported it, including those who had helped the initial ill-fated case. He was rightly proud when T.S. Eliot subscribed £25. On appeal Kavanagh won, at least to the extent that his costs in the earlier case were borne by the defendants. But too much damage had been done. Years earlier, when Oliver St John Gogarty had sued him for libel and won, he had gone prematurely grey and partly bald as a result of the traumas and ordeals of that experience. Shortly after the publication of *The Green Fool* in 1938, Oliver

St John Gogarty brought an action against the publisher, Michael Joseph. The passage that had angered Gogarty was one in which Kavanagh, freshly arrived in Dublin and paying his literary compliments, calls on Gogarty at his house in Ely Place; the door is opened and here, in Kavanagh's words: ' I mistook Gogarty's white-robed maid for his wife—or mistress. I expected every poet to have a spare wife.'

Gogarty was awarded £100 damages and the book ordered to be withdrawn. It was not republished until five years after the author's death. Gogarty is later alleged to have claimed that what really hurt him about the passage was, not so much the slight to his wife, but the suggestion that he had only *one* mistress! This time, twenty years afterwards, a more deadly illness was to visit Kavanagh. To understand the madness that allowed him to rush once more into the breach of law, we have to remember that, like a lot of the Irish (and Irish country people in particular) he was extremely litigious—one of the more deadly Hibernian sins.

His father was a hob-lawyer, mingling his skills as accordion importer and shoemaker with that of lay attorney, and at which, by all accounts, he was an ' unqualified ' success. He had a copy of *Pears' Encyclopaedia* for 1891, which contained in the supplement instructions for making out a will and testament, some advice on *torts*, and such toothsome morsels concerning ownership as ' breach of warranty in the sale of a cow '. This was to be his (and, I fear, Paddy's) Law Library and Kings Inns rolled into one!

The illness that followed the libel suit very nearly proved fatal; a malignant growth necessitated the removal of one of his lungs. However, a successful operation was performed after which there was a long period of convalescence which, it can be said, he enjoyed. He was obliged to stay in hospital and, as a result of the experience, grew to like being helpless and having things done for him and decisions made. It was not far removed from his ante-natal dream. He would look forward, from now on, to his fairly frequent visits to hospital.

Indeed, on one occasion when we were together in Mooney's in Baggot Street, he just decided on the spur of the moment to admit himself. There seemed no specific reason for admitting him to the Royal City of Dublin Hospital, but a host of unnamed maladies of which, one supposes, *weltschmerz* was one, and *taedium vitae,* another. Anyhow, he simply lay on a table in the accident admissions ward, refusing to leave until he was taken in as a patient.

After the law case, the illness and the miraculous re-birth by the canal, it could be said that the storm of his life was over; that he had survived the reefs and the shoals. True, the seas had knocked his old hull about, but she was still afloat and would continue her course, though less impatiently, into the more placid regions where long calms prevail.

By now he had earned the recognition of his peers and the admiration and respect of the laity. He appreciated their avowals of fealty. As an established man of letters of some eminence (at least in the English-speaking world) he could afford to relax. His books were being reprinted; *Tarry Flynn* not only became a paperback, but a popular Abbey play (I can still hear his grunts of approval for Donal McCann's randy interpretation of his young self in that production); McGibbon and Kee brought out the *Collected Pruse* and the *Collected Poems.* He gave lectures and television interviews. In short, success had arrived, late certainly and somewhat down-at-heel (for the bogey of finance continued to haunt)—but better late than never. This last eight years became a final independent passage in his life which had had a recognizable beginning, middle and end—like the coda that marks the end of a musical composition. There was a somewhat luxurious melancholy about the period. Autumnal you might say.

He travelled much in those years, making several trips to America. On one of these he visited Ezra Pound in St Elizabeth's Hospital near Washington (DC), the asylum where the poet was incarcerated for many years following his imprisonment in an animal's cage in Pisa, after the American liberation of Italy. After the visit, he stopped a taxi in the vicinity of the asylum with the intention of returning to his hotel. The driver, convinced that he himself was an escaped patient, tried to soothe and calm him, even going so far as to pull up at the first police precinct on the pretence of ' enquiring the way to the hotel ', from the local cops. Years later, after Pound had attended the funeral of T.S. Eliot in London (1967), he crossed the Irish Sea to visit Mrs George Yeats (the widow of W.B.). He refused to speak to the press, let alone give an interview. According to Mrs Yeats, the only Irish person he even so much as mentioned was Paddy Kavanagh. He had not forgotten.

More frequently now, Kavanagh visited London, a place which was very close to his heart. It was a city in which he had never suffered as he believed he had in Dublin. Many of his friends were there: poets, writers and painters—George Barker, David Wright, John Heath-Stubbs, Lucien Freud, the ' Roberts '—the crowd in the Plough, the George, the Cumberland Stores and the Queen's Elm. To them he would sing (at the drop of a hat) ' Lord Ullin's Daughter ' and other favourites. Kavanagh's London is every bit as valid an entity as his Inniskeen and his Baggotonia.

Robert MacBryde and his partner, Robert Colquohn, were a homosexual, married couple, much loved everywhere and, being inseparable, were known as ' The Roberts '! Like all married couples they quarrelled a good deal. Although they were distinguished painters of the wartime neo-Romantic school, deservedly renowned, their drinking habits placed too heavy a burden on their financial resources so that they were always at their wits' ends to make ends meet. I remember one grand row in the *Caves de France* which ended up with Colquohn reading off MacBryde like an RSM in the Argyll and Sutherlands. With the whole bar listening eagerly, he eventually brought the matter to a close by thundering, ' Ma father was rrright. Yer nothing but a whoooarr . . .'

For a brief period Paddy shared a house in Dublin with

MacBryde (who was shortly afterwards killed in a street accident) and Richard O'Riordan. Robert told me that one night he found Paddy critically examining a small tin of peas in the kitchen. ' I said to him,' said Robert, in his strong Scottish brogue, ' " Would you nay think weel to have yon fine noorishing mulligatawny sooop instead o' thim farthy wee peas that'll do ye damn all guid? " '

' It's for to pee into, the tin; not for the peas in it I want it—in case I'm short taken during the night', was the poet's exasperated, though pragmatic, reply.

On a fine summer's afternoon, he lay down in front of the members' stand at the Phoenix Park races and slept. Maybe, like the boxer who said, ' We wuz robbed. We should-ah stood in bed,' he should-ah remained asleep, for it was a disastrous day for the punters. Having clocked up one final loser on the last race, bringing the grand total to seven— which, in fact, was the number run—he was in no mood to tarry, despite the fact that the Artane Boys' Band, from their podium above the two-shilling tote booths, was dispensing the National Anthem to a multitude of silent race-goers. Paddy, indifferent to patriotic stances, proceeded with his loping gait (not unlike Groucho Marx's, many thought) to make good his retreat from this field of battles lost. An irate nationalist who saw treason in this, blocked his path and demanded what the hell he thought he was doing by not standing at attention for the 'Soldier's Song'?

' Is it that ould rubbishy come-all-ye by Brendan Behan's grandmother? Will ya bugger off outa me way.' The National Anthem (*The Soldier's Song*) was actually written by Brendan's uncle, Peadar Kearney. He was the author of many well-known songs including *The Bold Fenian Men*. Confusing uncle with grandmother may have been deliberate. Getting names mixed up on purpose was a well-known Kavanagh ploy.

The loping Kavanagh gait became a galloping retreat as the fiery patriot, appalled by these blasphemies, threatened to ' have his guts for garters.' Increasing his stride, our hero only managed to gain the main gate of the racecourse, for by now there was a small but hostile crowd in hot pursuit. Fortunately for him, a fellow-countyman of his, a neighbour and friend, Chief Superintendent Quinn of the Gárda Síochána, happened to be just outside the gates supervising the regulation of traffic. By engaging the Superintendent in earnest conversation relating to the parishes and baronies of Monaghan (until the hour of crisis was passed and the mob mollified) disaster was averted.

The following day, he had forgotten this part of the saga, but remembered the incident of sleeping on the grass; particularly as the *Irish Times* had a photograph of him thus reclined, spread across the front page.

' I'm too sick to sue,' he groaned with resignation.

Just before Christmas of 1963, I was producing Beckett's *Happy Days* in Joan Littlewood's Theatre Workshop in Stratford East in London. Paddy wished to see it. I left a couple of tickets in Sean Treacy's pub, the aforesaid Queen's Elm, also instructions as to how to get out there if he should so decide to use London's underground transport system. I tried to make these as brief and succinct as possible:

From Kensington Station take the Piccadilly Line in the Cockfosters direction, change at Holborn to the Central Line, making sure it is aimed for Ongar, thence to Stratford East; *or* take the District Line from South Kensington in the Upminster Bridge direction, pausing to change for (again) the Central Line at Mile End and once more straight on to Stratford. On arrival at the station, it is but a piffling mile-and-a-half walk to the theatre where a warm welcome will await you in the nearby Green Man.

It was with some nausea that he listened to this rigmarole— for him, crossing a road was a prodigious journey . . . Eventually he was moved to intervene.

' Tell Ryan the account is closed.'

But it was far from being so, despite my having to have

my little joke. It recalled for me what the poet, Ginsberg, had said in New York when he was thirsty for drinking company and meeting Paddy by chance on Fifth Avenue, only then to discover that the Irish poet, for once (in an unconscionable while), was not in the mood for drinking, roared back:

' O.K. Kavanagh, goodbye FOREVER ! '

Once in ' Hell's Kitchen ', a Soho-type neighbourhood off Times Square, he had seen just about as much of the seamy side, that is to say, the Ginsberg side, as he had stomach for. He would give me an imitation of the typical stance that the barman would take in any of the seedy taverns of the district when trouble was a-brewing and the inevitable ' *let it ride* ' which was said with a considerable amount of compressed vehemence. He didn't think it was really his scene.

Dede and John Farrely were good friends and hosts to him in New York. Once he took a holiday with them in Nice; though he loved them he equated that city with everything he loathed. He would, in reverie, fantasize about himself in the role of a district justice: someone would be before him for deplorable, lewd conduct.

' If I have said it once, I've said it a hundred times from this bench,' he would thunder to amazed customers of bookies' shops and bars, ' I'll not tolerate this blackguardly conduct. Don't think you can come before me and expect to get away with a paltry five-shilling fine. If I see you in that dock before me again I can promise you not less than three weeks in Nice! Not a very nice prospect, eh? What? Think on it. Ponder it...'

On Bloomsday, 1967, he unveiled the door of number seven Eccles Street (the real home of Joyce's friend, John Francis Byrne, ' Cranly ' in *The Portrait* ... and the fictitious home of Leopold and Molly Bloom in *Ulysses*). I had saved this door from the wreckers when the building was demolished and transferred it to the vestibule of the Bailey. Milo O'Shea, who had just completed the role of Bloom in Joseph Strick's film version of the classic, was also there. Paddy concluded his speech with the following lines, words which (with the exception of a tiny poem he wrote, under great duress, for Hayden Murphy's *Broadsheet*), may have been his last written composition:

> The first and last time a piece of valid native propaganda for the Joyce thing happened was on the fiftieth anniversary of Bloomsday in 1954, when a few of us, led by Myles na gCopaleen, John Ryan, Tony Cronin, myself and a cousin of Joyce, hired four unrehabilitated cabs and pilgrimed to the Tower, at a time when it was neither popular nor profitable, to quote Myles. We had drinks in Michael Scott's and returned via Sandymount Strand. No press cameras recorded our travels. Indeed we were the object of some jeering in the various pubs we visited. However, two cameras did record our pilgrimage, Elinor O'Brien, as she then was, made a complete record of our expedition and John Ryan did a film job on it. And one of the most memorable takes of that film was of the incomparable Myles pissing on Sandymount Strand.
>
> And that's how it was before the American bit the dog 'til he laid the golden eggs. And now it merely is left to me to declare this holy door irrevocably - - - - - - Shut. And to call upon Mr Milo Bloom O'Shea to address the assembled multitudes.

Paddy married that same month Kathleen Barry Maloney, whom he had known from his London trips—she had worked in publishing there for several years. It was a marriage of true friends. What a pity that there was so little time left for them to enjoy it.

Late in November of that year he died. He was sixty-two. A week before his death the Abbey players were giving a performance of *Tarry Flynn* in the town of Dundalk. He asked me to drive him up there, which I did. We took the same road that the young man had walked over forty years before. He told me again how as a boy he had walked to Dublin from Inniskeen, yet only crossed the lands of three men. The three men's lands are now, I suppose, the lands of many men; perhaps only the Earl of Mountcharles of that mighty triumvirate retains any worth talking about, but even then a brisk ten minutes' walk would put you across his territory. We stopped at a few pubs on the way that Paddy knew—but it wasn't the best time. You see, the Fianna Fáil Árd Fheis was on up in Dublin and all the publicans were at that. We dropped into Dan MacNello's pub in Inniskeen—an old friend. The pub is the social centre of Inniskeen. Not far from it is the bridge over the lovely Fane river ' one of the best trout rivers in Ireland ', where Paddy as a boy had helped to poach the great salmon. We had a drink or two there with some of the actors. Pat Laffan had a camera, so that there is for posterity a photograph of us all in MacNello's. In the last picture, Paddy looks like Moses; and did he not, like the patriarch, show us the promised land? And, like the prophet, fail to attain it himself? More than fifty years earlier, he remembered his father going into the same MacNello's and ordering a ton of flour. It was August 1914, the day the great war broke out. ' The Germans will bate the world ', a customer had brightly observed, and a boy carried the memory. A week later the price of flour had doubled!

We spent the night in the Imperial Hotel in Dundalk. He was staying on the next day to see the play, while I was returning to Dublin. In the morning I met him in the dining room. Downstairs in the bar he ordered a large smathán of Scotch— his favourite drink—and worried because he hadn't left the girl in the dining room a tip. He saw her and gave her five shillings. I got up to go.

' I'm off now, Paddy. Goodbye ', I said.

' So long, John ', he replied. A large lone figure.

I never saw him again.

He died a few days later in a Dublin nursing home on the last day of November. It was a good month to die, he knew.

The ship that sailed so hopefully down the Fane had eventually joined the greater river, of which this was but the small Irish tributary; it in turn had widened imperceptibly and merged with the sea of history and the accumulation of the poetry of all the ages: the others—Homer, Pope, Shakespeare, Melville, Dante, Blake—were all about him now; and so a man on a desolate strand knows that the tide has quietly surrounded him with the waters, about which, until then, he had no inkling.

O commemorate me where there is water,
Canal water preferably, so stilly
Greeny at the heart of summer. Brother . . .
O commemorate me with no hero courageous
Tomb—just a canal-bank seat for the passer-by.

Paddy had written these lines (which were themselves inspired by a seat near Baggot Street Bridge, which was put up to the memory of Mrs Dermot O'Brien), and from them it was clear that it was his wish to be similarly remembered. Denis Dwyer and I decided, therefore, to do something about it. To this purpose we formed a committee of which he was chairman and I was honorary treasurer. The committee which was formed to set about the task consisted of Ronnie Walsh, T.P. McKenna, Pat Layde, Don Harris, Liam Brady, Siobhán McKenna, Garech de Brun, Senator and Mrs Eoin Ryan, Jim Fitzgerald, Michael Farrell and Sheila O'Grady (who was secretary). The first thing to do (before a split), we decided, was to set ourselves a time limit for the building and erection of the seat. The Irish can only work to deadlines. In the vapidness of unlimited time, their hopes and aspirations dissolve like the mists of the morning.

It was already December 1967, and we gave ourselves until 17 March 1968, St Patrick's Day, to complete our task. Our committee meetings used to be held on Sunday mornings in the Ormond, that hotel of shimmering and fugal Joycean memories, and were as businesslike as the conviviality of having drinks with friends on the Sabbath would allow.

Michael Farrell designed the seat, basing his scheme on a rough sketch I had done on a drip-mat on the bar of the Bailey. Denis Dwyer who, as chairman, would bring sudden order to a boisterous meeting by sternly bringing down, with a resounding thud, his four-pound lump hammer which he used as a gavel, was instrumental in finding the oak from which the seat was made. It had been felled in Meath a century before Paddy himself was born. The stone that forms the two uprights is of granite from the Dublin mountains. John Cullen, whose monumental works were in the heart of the Kavanagh Baggotonia, caused the words of the poem mentioned to be inscribed on the stone. The surrounding paving is of Liscarra slabs from the Burren in county Clare.

A fund to raise the money was organized and most generously subscribed to. Humble, unknown people sent money, and celebrities contributed. From Dan MacNello, who owned the pub in Inniskeen, came £5, and from Dr George Otto Simms, the Protestant Archbishop of Dublin, a similar sum. Lord Moyne sent £10, and the poet, John Heath-Stubbs sent a smaller but nonetheless welcome contribution. Looking back at the list I kept, I see the names of the former Chief Justice of Ireland, Cearbhall Ó Dálaigh, and the poet, David Wright, Lord Kilbracken, the 'Pope' O'Mahony, Micheál MacLiammóir, and the only politician that all sides loved, Donagh O'Malley, also Lord Killanin, Benedict Kiely, Seamus Murphy, RHA, and a hundred more. Their names are not forgotten; in another and more suitable place they will be inscribed for posterity.

We thought it would be a nice thing to have his old friend, John Betjeman, over for the opening and wrote to him inviting him to do so. He declined regretfully. He had other, more pressing, engagements. It was, eventually, on a gusty St Patrick's Day, unveiled as promised. To mark the event, Siobhán McKenna and members of the Abbey Theatre company read a selection of his poems. The readers included Patrick Laffan, Patrick Layde, T.P. McKenna, Michael

Hennessey and Niall Toibín. Then Aideen O'Kelly spoke the canal poem, but in such dreamy, limpid tones, I don't believe there can have been many dry eyes. I know there were tears in mine.

Finally, three priests, Fr Cyril Barrett, SJ, Fr Tom Stack and Fr Austin Flannery, OP, blessed the seat. It was gratifying that men of their calibre, fighters for good causes and friends of the arts, agreed to perform this simple ceremony, for the man we were remembering was a great artist and a great humanitarian.

Today we may linger on that seat and look down the lovely vista of the canal which he knew so well and which, when threatened with obliteration by the Corporation, so many of us fought to protect. It was, in its own city way, as lovely as the Fane was to him. You can idle where so often he did, remembering that it was here that he had his renewal —his rebirth. You may see the descendants of the swans that glided past him nodding their heads ' with many apologies.' But no longer, alas, a canal barge with argosies of peat from furthest Athy. But you may see the occasional family ' cruiser ' bobbing gently in the lock while the ' crew ' attend to the exacting business of opening and closing the cumbersome gates.

In the fulness of summer, when the poplars and beeches crowd the heavens with turbulent foliage, the skies, the trees, and water all seem to merge in one quivering unity. From his seat, you will see the waters of the canal falling ' Niagarously ' into the lock, and your vision, as you raise your head, will be led a half mile up the canal until it meets the winking eye of Eustace Bridge. Then, the immense beauty of it all touches the heart. At such a moment one may concede that some parnassian deity (a friend now of the poet) is presiding over the scene.

As for the seat? Lovers use it; typists take their lunch aboard it—when the weather permits; old men with dogs sit there and dream of the old days; homewardbound revellers rest their boozy limbs on its uncomplaining boards—men who have never heard of the poet. Others just sit on it, as I sometimes do, and simply remember Paddy Kavanagh.

If ever you go to Dublin town
In a hundred years or so
Sniff for my personality,
Is it Vanity's vapour now?

II

The Incomparable Myles

De Selby likens the position of a human on the earth to that of a man on a tight-wire who must continue along the wire or perish, being, however, free in all other respects. Movement in this restricted orbit results in the permanent hallucination known conventionally as 'life' with its innumerable concomitant limitations, afflictions and anomalies.

Flann O'Brien: *The Third Policeman*

Brian O'Nolan was three divinely humorous personae in one. He wrote under the names of Myles na gCopaleen (a character from Boucicault's play, *The Colleen Bawn*), Flann O'Brien and Brian Ó Nualláin. Hereinafter he will be referred to, by me, simply as Myles.

Patrick Kavanagh, who threw compliments about like a man with no arms (viz: 'Yeats? I could do without him . . .'), called him the 'incomparable'. He meant it—not in the effete way that Shaw applied it to Max Beerbohm—it was linked in his mind with 'irreplaceable'. Paddy survived Myles by a little more than a year, but even in that short period often remarked to me that there really was nobody left to talk to in Dublin now that Myles was gone. He was one of the few writers in whose company he was completely at ease; his respect for him was complete; he was his peer; like himself he had chosen the tougher going, the thinner air of Upper Parnassus, Dublin 14.

Myles was a prodigy. His erudition was frightening and indeed many were frightened by it. His knowledge of languages and the complexities and idiocies of semantics (he regarded Dinneen's Irish-English dictionary as an enduring comic masterpiece) was as deep and widespread as Joyce's. Indeed, the existence of Myles explodes any theory that Joyce's appearance on the Irish literary scene was a unique event, never to be in any way repeated, and in no way indicative of the true state of Irish letters.

Joyce knew and admired Myles' work, though never the twain, alas, were to meet. A well-thumbed copy of *At Swim-Two-Birds* was said to be found among Joyce's effects after his death. Myles' own attitude to Joyce is best summed up in his introductory essay to the book on Joyce and the Irish entitled *A Bash In The Tunnel,* an outrageously funny amalgam of faith in Joyce the writer and despair in Joyce the man. Had they met we might have got something a great deal more mordant and witty than, say, the disastrous meeting of Joyce and Proust—which was, however, not without unintended comic overtures itself.

Myles allowed that Joyce had a keener ear for dialogue than he. To illustrate his point, he gave me this example: In the Cyclops sequence of *Ulysses*, when our hero is emerging from Barney Kiernan's pub in Little Britain Street, one of the bystanders yells after him, ' Eh, mister! Your fly is open, mister!' It was the use of the *second* ' mister ' that showed Joyce for the subtle artificer that he was. Myles admitted that his ear couldn't have taken in so quintessentially a piece of Dublinese as that nuance. Another example he gave was in the Hades episode from the same book. To comfort the mourners at Paddy Dignam's funeral, the caretaker of Glasnevin cemetery (Mr John O'Connell) is telling them a funny yarn about the two Dubliners who visit the cemetery at night and drunkenly set out to find the tomb of an old crony of theirs, ' Mulcahy of the Coombe '. In time, and by dint of lighting many matches, they find the grave. The inscription on the tombstone confirms the fact that it is indeed the grave of their friend. However, looking up at the statue above, which happens to be that of the Sacred Heart, but failing to find corroboration therein, one of them opines, ' Not a bloody bit like the man. That's not Mulcahy,' says he, ' whoever done it.' ' Whoever done it ' is high Dublin idiom at its most hilarious. Again Myles was ready to acknowledge that he could not have essayed that one either.

Allowing Myles's modest appraisal of himself to be, by and large, correct (but only in this hair-splitting judgement—when it came to an impeccable ear for Dublin dialogue), we yet must surely allow him the second place or, to be scrupulously fair, a tie between himself and Sean O'Casey for that prize. True, the latter has given us the Covey, Joxer and Uncle Peter, but who are even this tremendous trio in comparison with Myles' single, all-purpose Dubliner, ' The Brother '?

This ' Brother ' is the archetypal Liffeysider. He is Dublin absolute and of the nadir. Like any true city-slicker, he is a know-all. Naturally he is also hob-lawyer, pub-philosopher and letter-to-the-editor writer on all civic matters. He is very quick with the repartee. Essentially humourless, he is the catalyst for an unending sequence of comic implosions that are centred upon his person. His many alarming encounters with the English language leave the latter bloody and, if not unbowed, less game for the next bout. In a sense O'Casey foretold the Brother—he rather suggests him, in a few bold strokes in the Covey, but Myles fills in the details, rounds off the man, gives him flesh and bones; in short presents him in three dimensions and immortalizes him. On another, more august end of the scale of human comedy, he gives us the ' da ', otherwise Sir Myles of Great Hall, Santry. (Even ' Santry ' is a kind of Dublin ' joke ' word. Cities, like families, have ' in ' jokes.) But ' the Brother ', Dublin's Everyman, is Myles' most singular gift to the comic literature of our times—possibly all times.

The Dubliner of the post-natal Free State and the subsequent Eire, as indeed the entire ethos of the Plain People of Ireland during that first heady morning of Nationhood, their manners and mores, vices and virtues, the incredible posturings and grotesque ' patriotic ' antics of the founding fathers, the pro-

K

liferating tangle of bureaucracy that envelops the *nouveau*-Irish are, by him, recorded as lovingly and faithfully as Joyce, a half century earlier, recalled his own post-Parnellite, Edwardian Dublin. Both, in their writings, have preserved their city from the indifferent ravages of time. No city was ever better served by her stepsons.

One does not seek for analogues between Myles and Joyce. Uninvited they continue to present themselves. Neither was a true Dubliner—despite each one's individual passion for the city and its citizens. Joyce was only a first generation jackeen, his father being from Cork and his mother from Longford, while Myles was born in the county of Tyrone. These places are about as far as you can get from Dublin in a straight line. But they were able to see it with new, fresh, young eyes. Both were pontifical in their utterances. They spoke *ad urbi et orbi*.

In physical appearance, Myles might have stepped out of the pages of *At Swim-Two-Birds*—a figment of his own imagination. He was small but not dapper, while his forehead was immense by comparison with the rest of his head. Relentless eyes glinted beneath dense, bushy eyebrows, but prominent 'Bugs Bunny' teeth comically contradicted their stern message, so that he often gave an appearance of demented benignity, such was the odd conjunction of meekness and ferocity in his features.

His garments were those of the 'chronic' medical student of the far-off thirties. Not that his formidable mental apparatus permitted him to belong to that category—it was just that he hankered for sartorial identification, at least, with all his boozing pals of the Green Bar, Hartigan's, Dwyer's and my uncle's place, the Stirling, in those never-to-be-forgotten days.

Myles had reached the zenith of his powers while still a student of University College. His life, thereafter, was a diminuendo. No wonder he yearned for a past that had so many good things going for it—youth, acclaim, vigour, promise and the good health to permit the enjoyment of sustained carousal!

He had the most curious way of walking. His legs seemed to be taking off on independent courses—unrelated to the desired destination of the rest of the body. In later years, when somewhat the worse for wear, I have seen him ' hove-to ', that is to say, maintaining position but making slight headway in a sea of pedestrians, while apparently going astern. This complicated manoeuvre was always conducted with the special gravity that the slightly inebriated give to their ambulatory occasions. Bureaucracy fascinated him—he had, himself, risen to its heights in the civil service, so he knew its internal workings well. He was the scourge of bad bye-laws, petty tyrannies and officialese, either English or Irish. As often as not, he battered his head in vain against that wall of ' pluterperfect imperturbability '—but the wall took some heavy blows too. For all that he only achieved about one per cent of success in the thousands of wrongs that he set out to put right, *yet,* entrenched bureaucracy was never quite so secure or complacent again. The fear of his ridicule still hangs over the corridors of power.

He regarded himself, primarily, as a citizen. Matters unconnected with the day-to-day affairs of the metropolis he did not consider to lie within his provenance. Mind you, to alleviate such mundaneness, he also presided over his self-created and self-perpetuating one-man *Academie Irlandaise* which was chiefly concerned with the preservation of the purity of our first and second languages (in what order, was your own prerogative) and in this sphere he wielded unchallenged power.

When he descended from these giddy etymological heights it was to scold the Dublin Corporation and put some form of manners on its employees. Future savants may well be perplexed by the frequent references to Andy Clarkin's clock and its permanent ' stopped ' condition, which crop up in *Cruiskeen Lawn,* Myles' daily column in the *Irish Times.* Clarkin was, at the time, Lord Mayor of Dublin. By occupation he was a coal merchant. The clock referred to was the large one hanging outside and advertising his premises. Civic-spirited Myles drew Andy's attention (and that of the public) to this uncivic state

of affairs in his column. Andy, alas, failed to jump to it and
have his clock repaired. For this he was mercilessly lampooned
in the column. Eventually Myles only had to use the one word
ACCISS (Andy Clarkin's Clock Is Still Stopped) to get his
message across. Andy, meanwhile, had decided to do nothing
about the clock in order not to please Myles. About such
minutiae (as Churchill might say) revolves man's destiny.
Myles, in turn, became more and more disgruntled by Andy's
obduracy—so that in the end the whole business became bitter,
futile and ultimately boring. Clarkin, although a career politician and considered by most to be a humourless one to boot,
nevertheless had the wisdom to make a commercial virtue out
of a journalistic necessity and permitted photographers from
the *Irish Times* to take pictures of his now celebrated clock
from a wide variety of angles. In due course these were printed,
publicity never does you any harm—be you vote catcher or
coal peddler—so Andy got the last laugh.

Did ever anyone belong more than the good Myles himself
to ' that caucus up there in City Hall '? He would have been at
home exchanging civilities with the city's fathers, for their daily
trivia was the raw material of so much of his comedy. He
should have held the title of Honorary Associate Alderman
just as ' Pope ' O'Mahony should have been, by presidential
appointment, Honorary Senator and Genealogist in Ordinary
to the Oireachtas. A subsequent minister, Patrick Smith, however, was not so tolerant and Myles found himself on the
retired list of the Department a good deal sooner than he had
anticipated. Even then, had it not been for the intervention
of a senior officer, a colleague and friend, he would not have
had the benefit of the small pension which was eventually
given him.

As he never lost his hankering for his student cronies and
jollification, he never lost his undergraduate iconoclasm nor
tempered his reformist zeal to the ever more congenial circumstances that his inevitable climb in the civil service yielded.
When we see the rioting students of today, we may well ask

ourselves ' where are the similarly rioting students of seven years ago?' 'Settled down as well-off doctors, dentists, engineers, lawyers, civil servants, no doubt', we uneasily find ourselves replying. Not so with Myles na gCopaleen. He became more youthfully ardent in the fight against the oppressor's wrongs as time progressed.

When he was in ' the full fit of his health ', as they say, he pulled off some great pranks. These were not purely student nor inconsequential, but had a purpose, a definable object—in most cases that of showing-up the self-evident ambiguities of most regulations and the asinine premises of so many laws. Bad English and consequently bad draughtsmanship were, as ever, the principal culprits. Typical was the time he borrowed an engineless car from a friend who owned a garage. With the help of friends he pushed it out one night and ' parked ' it in a prominent downtown position. Next day the car was by then, thanks to such imprecise parking, the subject of much garda surveillance. Myles feigning advanced drunkenness, putting on for the purpose a quite hilarious pantomime (a drunk's drunk), was very quickly nabbed by the police. The exact charge against him related to his attempting to drive a *mechanically-propelled vehicle* while under the influence of alcohol. He, of course, was able to prove that the machine, being without an engine, was not a mechanically-propelled vehicle, *qua* vehicle!

Another jape I often heard mentioned, which he was supposed to have perpetrated, came to pass on an occasion when the guards actually *did* get him for driving a proper mechanically-propelled vehicle while under the influence. They were holding him pending the arrival of the police doctor (this, of course, was in pre-breathalizer days) when he suddenly produced a half bottle of whiskey from his pocket, draining the contents there and then before the eyes of a dumb-founded desk-sergeant!

It was a source of wonder the way he managed to provide something new for his daily column and yet, whenever I met him, he could furnish further, original material—(for my ears only?) which, perhaps for deeper purposes, could not appear in print. It was invariably vastly comic.

I recall a fragment of an epic—though the story itself is lost (who wants a plot anyhow?)—I still have the salient points. The action takes place near the Dublin Corporation Livestock Market in Prussia Street. The *dramatis personae* are small farmers and cattle drovers. Their early morning labours finished, they adjourned to the hotel nearby for a hearty breakfast of steak and whiskey. It is about seven o'clock (old time) on a freezing January morning. Even in the diningroom the men's breath hangs like salted ling. Requests for more coal to ' bring on the fire ' go unheeded. In exasperation they throw the handsome, walnut, eight-day, chiming centrepiece into the fire and, to keep it company, a small mahogany *bureau-plat* with tulipwood veneer. ' I don't know what sort of a shower is going to the markets these days at all,' complains the aggrieved proprietor later to Myles, ' I don't believe they're drovers at all—more like bloody herds.'

Another tale of many outrageous complexities which had me clinging onto some bar counter, concerned an attempt to set up a motor assembly in Dublin before the war. It seems that one, Kelly, had a bicycle shop. Things were only going so-so until a great inspiration came upon him (like religion came to Paddy in the chapel)—he would do what the other founding fathers had done, get the concession to assemble a particular make of car and, thanks to our immense tariff wall, sit back with what amounted to a licence to print money!

Of course, by this time all the well-known brands of cars had been cornered by the early birds. Kelly, a latecomer, had to content himself with some rather obscure East-European model. Finally, he ran one to earth, the little-known Bratis-lavian automobile—the ' Rosteneimer '; the ' big R.M. ', as it was called. Telegrams were dispatched to Herr Rosteneimer himself, inviting him to appoint Kelly his sole concessionary in the Irish Free State.

Intrigued though suspicious, Rosteneimer decided to investigate in person. There was no Dublin Airport, or indeed, Aer Lingus then, but he flew in just the same, landing his own Focke-Wulf on the greensward at Baldonnel, the Irish Army flying field. Kelly was on hand to greet him and to spirit him away in his gleaming Hispano-Suiza—borrowed for the occasion, needless to remark. A banquet was laid on at the North Star Hotel—tinned grapefruit, tomato soup, roast chicken, ham, and colcannon, sherry-trifle and different coloured wines, i.e., red and white. There he met the other, putative, directors of Rosteneimer Fabriken (I. F. S.) Ltd.,— Kelly's three sons, as shady a lot as you might encounter in a day's walk.

Herr Rosteneimer was a man of few words. Occasionally he would adjust his monocle and say ' ja ', or, shrugging dubious shoulders, relinquish an ' Ah, so . . . ' The banquet duly consumed, all parties adjourned to the site where the great car assembly works was going to be erected. After a tortuous journey through streets broad and narrow, they ended up in some small alley off Little Britain Street. Kelly produces a key and opens the door of a corrugated iron lean-to shed in an advanced state of decomposition—its sole occupants a venerable lady's upright bicycle and a one-eyed tom-cat. ' Vat iss diss, den '? queries Herr Rosteneimer. ' This is going to be where we assemble the cars ', replies Kelly. ' Ah so . . . ', muses Herr Rosteneimer. Then he takes out the monocle, slowly cleans it on his silk monogrammed handkerchief, screws it back into his eye, glares terribly at Kelly and his clan. ' It iss in mine arse!' hisses Herr Rosteneimer by way of final valediction.

I met him often socially in those days. His haunts were many and varied but principally I would come across him in Neary's (where the ' common hangman ', according to Behan, drank); but also at *Doheny and Nesbitt's, The Dolphin, The Pearl, The Palace, The White Horse, Mulligan's* of Poolbeg Street, *Cheerio Ryan's* (in Dun Laoire), *The Morgue* in Templeogue, *Matt Smith's* of Stepaside, *The Dead Man Murray's, Gerry Byrne's* of Galloping Green, *The Bleeding Horse, Ye Olde*

Grinding Younge, The Brazen Head, The Winter Garden Palace, Dolly Fossett's, The Ouzel Galley, and *The Widow Flavin's* in Sandyford. A man could easily die of cirrhosis in the fair city without having seen even half of its seven hundred odd pubs. Before that gloomy knight joins the company most have seen but a tenth of that number.

Our first literary association came about when he offered me a short story which nobody else would publish, including the *Irish Times* which, as we have noted, featured a daily column of his. It was a piece entitled ' The Martyr's Crown ' and had to do with a singular phenomenon—the man who was *born* for Ireland.

The gist of the matter (and of the story) was that way back in the time of the old days when the Black and Tan war was at its fiercest, some of the ' boys ' on the run were given refuge in the house of a Mrs Clougherty on the South side. She was a lady of exemplary piety who had all hands (Protestant, Catholic, Jew) on their knees to say the Rosary by nine o'clock. In addition she was a stern and unflinching daughter of Erin and a headquarters Staff Captain in the Cumann na mBan.

Came a day when there was a fearful commotion outside in the street and the boys, peeping through the blinds, found themselves surrounded by ' lurries ' full of Black and Tans— armed, one and all, to the teeth, while an officer pounded the door lustily with the butt end of a service Webley.

Unruffled and ignoring the ashen-faced boys, the virtuous and proper Mrs Clougherty, having ' foostered ' for a moment in front of the mirror, gave them a last look as much as to say, ' Shut up you lousers ', and made straight for the hall door.

From their hideaway the boys could hear Mrs Clougherty engaging the Lieutenant in conversation. Though her speech had lost its refined ' blas ' (for she had now substituted this with the ' guttiest ' Dublin accent this side of Moore Street); none-theless it had a beguiling tone to it that her normal locution lacked. Further, through a keyhole they could discern that she was fingering, meaningfully, the top button of her lurex sateen blouse. By-and-by they heard the drawingroom door close softly behind the Lieutenant of the Auxiliaries and the Staff Captain of the Cumann na mBan.

After an eternity another door, but this time the hall door, was heard to slam, followed by further commotion; this time it was the din of the 'lurries' departing. It was a subdued household that knelt down to the Rosary (a little earlier than usual) that night; but the boys were safe . . .

The ensuing progeny of this crucial liaison, this brief political encounter, was a good-looking fellow, somewhat stuck up in his ways, a likely lad with airs who could be seen years later strolling about the streets.

> And he, of course, was that collectors item, not just one of your countless numbers who had merely died for Ireland but one who had actually been born for Mother Eirinn! No medals for it—but what a distinction!

Into the pellucid and pietistic waters of Irish chauvinism when it was launched this story took on the appearance of an armed torpedo run amok. It was considered particularly sacrilegious because of the saintly character then universally attributed to revolutionary Irish ladies. In order that a title becoming their status but without having imperialistic overtones might be given them, and which as a bonus would allow them also to dispense with the English prefix 'Mrs' and the more degrading Irish 'Bean Uí' (meaning 'woman of') it was spontaneously decided that they should be all called 'Madame'. It had a French revolutionary tinkle to it but was accorded only to outstanding female nationalists, or patriotic feminists of great pith and moment. They were a very formidable herd of sacred cows and at the time of publlication many were still alive. Apart from the great Madame Maud Gonne herself there also dwelt amongst us Madame Rogers, Madame Toto Cogley, Madame D'Espard and Madame Kirkwood Hackett. And of course if there had been a real Mrs Clougherty she would by now have been Madame Clougherty and the dam of a long line of TD's. Or would she?

Occasionally, when he was not feeling himself, as it were,

and his hand was none too steady, I would drive him home in the evening and type his morning column to his dictation. He would declaim it fluently without interruption, hesitancy or revision and without notes, as though (for his eyes were fixed on seeming space) he were reading from a teleprompt. It was a virtuoso performance which made me think that his mind was a great chamber containing serried ranks of Cruiskeen Lawns ready to step forward on a command.

He and I worked on several projects. Jointly we put together the James Joyce special number of *Envoy* which was the genesis of *A Bash In the Tunnel*. Another of our ventures was to organize the first ' Bloomsday '. On 16 June 1954, the fiftieth anniversary of the day on which the events of Joyce's *Ulysses* took place, we decided to commemorate it by covering as much of the original ground as the book had charted.

There were still a few horse cabs plying the streets for hire in those days (the one-horse ' brougham ' was as peculiar to Dublin in Joyce's day as the hansom cab was to London in Conan Doyle's); so we chartered two splendidly decrepit examples, all black and verdigris, straw stuffing bursting through the upholstery and the indispensable ' jarveys ' with watery eyes and noses that they had spent a lot of time and money colouring.

We agreed that the company should consist of ourselves, A.J. (Con) Levanthal, Anthony Cronin, Patrick Kavanagh and Tom Joyce. Con Levanthal, being Jewish, was to symbolize Bloom; Cronin, the young poet, his surrogate offspring Stephen; Myles enjoined Simon Dedalus and Martin Cunningham; I was Myles Crawford (for I had been an editor); Kavanagh—the muse, and Tom Joyce, The Family; for he was a cousin of James—a dentist who had, in fact, never read *Ulysses*!

Our ' pilgrimace ' (to use Andrew Cass's expression—in our case most applicable I think, being a pilgrimage, a grimace and, to some extent, a disgrace), departed from the Martello Tower, from the parapet of which Buck Mulligan presides over the opening ceremonies of the book. This is the ' Tele-

machus' chapter. Our plan thereafter was to take in the
'Nestor' episode in nearby Dalkey, proceed directly to the
'Proteus' section of Sandymount Strand, thus to Eccles Street
(the beginning of the 'Calypso' chapter) and then in one broad
swathe, take in the 'Lotus Eaters' (Westland Row and
environs), 'Hades' (Glasnevin cemetery), 'Aeolus' (the *Free-
man's Journal* office—we proposed to substitute the *Irish Times*
for that defunct organ), pausing for lunch and liquid refreshments at 'Lestrygonians' (Davy Byrnes, the Bailey).

Our leisurely afternoon would be taken up with 'Scylla and
Charybdis' (The National Library), 'The Wandering Rocks'
(no fixed abode—so our plan for that was to ascend Nelson's
Pillar and drink toasts in Cork whiskey to the four quadrants
of Dublin), afterwards to the Ormond Hotel for the interlude
of the 'Sirens', and then to the nearest extant pub in the
vicinity of that dried up well, Barney Kiernan's 'Court of
Appeal' for the explosive 'Cyclops' scene—back quickly to
Sandymount for 'Nausicaa', then onwards to Holles Street
Hospital (a passing glance only) for the 'Oxen of the Sun',
thence to Mabbot and Mecklenburg Streets—Dublin's vanished
'nighttown'—for a moment's silence for Bella Cohen, then for
'Eumaeus'—a late-night cup of coffee at some stall (the cab-
men's shelter is also gone) and finally to number seven Eccles
Street for some conviviality and to celebrate the return to
'Ithaca' and 'Penelope', thus ending our Odyssey.

Well, it was a good try . . . a cheering stirrup cup from
Michael Scott sent us merrily on our way. From the Martello
Tower our two-carriage progress soon became a cavalcade as
numerous other vehicles tagged on behind. More pubs were
visited *en route* than even the most faithful adherence to the
Joycean master-plan demanded. By the time we reached the
purlieus of Duke Street ('Lestrygonians'), communications
became unreliable, transport broke down and the strict order
of procedure was permitted to lapse. If we could have delayed
this ossification to the 'Circe' episode it would have been more
in accordance with the structure of *Ulysses,* but nonetheless,

a great time was had by all. For history, I recorded the event on a colour movie which still brings back, in a few tantalizing moments, much of the flavour of that enchanting day.

The early part of our progress was, as I say, a reasonably stately affair and while, in retrospect, it is somewhat hazy, I clearly remember the dulcet tones of Cronin as he warbled the melodies of Tom Moore—the great *Believe Me If* and the sublime *Ah-ja-Pay-ill Muene* to mention but two. All agreed that these were the songs that Joyce himself would have liked sung, for indeed were they not the songs he sang so well with that fine, light, Irish tenor voice of his (a present from the da)?

Jogging along in our brougham, Myles told us how he had once gone to an Irish club in London, the membership of which was confined to university graduates. It was a very important Hibernian occasion, possibly St Patrick's night; that sort of thing. The club's concert hall was heavy with smoke and full of the sound of breaking bottles and noises as if people were happy. Someone who felt that the cup of human happiness was still not altogether filled was calling a drunken dentist to render his party piece. After much coaxing he was finally persuaded and somewhat unsteadily addressed himself to a large upright piano which had the words ' Eireann Go Bragh ' on the front, inscribed in fretwork.

After some introductory arpeggios on the butt-burned, yellowing ivories, our man, head tilted back, eyes narrowed, permitted his fingers to feel their way lovingly through the opening bars of *Oft In The Stilly Night*. Alas, the sweet melancholy of the melody must have proved too seductive, for in no time our pianist was seen to slump on top of the keyboard, a broken man. His undulatory collapse produced a wave-like movement which, in turn, unleashed a tremendous chromatic tidal wave and an RRRRHHHHHeeiiiK! from the creaky piano. At last, when the tumult subsided, the dentist, his head now recumbent on the key of C natural, could be heard, between sobs, as it were, keening ' O you who-arr Moo-arr, you who-arr Moo-arr . . . ' With this reluctant tribute to our national bard, Tom Moore, the lacrymose dentist finally collapsed.

Somewhere around Blackrock, on the main funeral route from Dublin to Dean's Grange Cemetery, lies a tavern, and there we had cause to pause for yet further refreshment. Perhaps it was the sound of our horses and carriages without, or just the sombre appearance of Myles (for he was wearing one of those black homburg hats he dubbed ' County Manager '), or merely the fact that he usually had funeral parties at about this time, that caused the landlord to approach us. He took Myles' hand to offer condolence. ' Nobody too close, I trust?' he queried hopefully. ' Just a friend,' replied Myles quietly, ' fellow by the name of Joyce—James Joyce . . .' meanwhile ordering another hurler of malt. ' James Joyce, . . .' murmured the publican thoughtfully, setting the glass on the counter, ' not the plastering contractor from Wolfe Tone Square?' ' *Naaahh* . . .' grunted Myles impatiently, ' the writer '. ' Ah! the *sign* writer ', cried the publican cheerfully, glad and relieved to have got to the bottom of this mystery so quickly, ' little Jimmy Joyce from Newtown Park Avenue, the sign writer, sure wasn't he only sitting on that stool there on Wednesday last week—wait, no, I'm a liar, it was ona Tuesday.'

' No!' Myles thundered, ' the *writer*. The wan that wrut the famous buke—" Useless " '. ' Ah, I see,' said the bewildered publican, and then more resignedly, ' I suppose we all have to go one day ', and resumed the drawing of my pint. ' Aye,' said Paddy Kavanagh, ' that's the way it is with some; more with others . . .'

Myles is gone. And gone too is the realization of many plans, for death came hurrying to greet him just as he seemed ready to embark on a second period of creativity. How fecund this might have been can only be surmised from a plan he discussed with me of writing an opera based on the Irish ballad ' The Palatine's Daughter '. A detail of the stage directions that I recall was the inclusion and use of real cannon in the prologue. We also talked of the idea of revising his comedy *Faustus Kelly*. I wanted to produce it as it stood but he was quite adamant about the last act being rewritten. Characteristically, he did not blame the Abbey Theatre for the poor showing of the play which they had given briefly many years before, but himself for writing it less than perfectly. As it was, there just wasn't the time to complete the new version.

He told me of another fantasy then incubating in his tireless brain. It concerned an American lady of untold wealth whose plan for the salvation of Ireland was to cover the entire island with a dense carpet of starch-yielding sago trees, which would supply the aborigines with a potato-substitute requiring no husbandry and which would be self-perpetuating. An Irish Arcadia would surely ensue. Or would it? The epic was to be called *The Sago Saga*.

One of the last times I saw him was on the opening night of the play adaptation of *The Dalkey Archive* at the Gate Theatre, entitled *When The Saints Come Cycling In*. In a curtain speech he told of how he was somewhat worried that he might have given offence to Augustine, by virtue of the numerous flippancies and irreverences concerning the saint that abound in the work. He was, he claimed, being visited by innumerable plagues, any of which might well be the last. Shortly afterwards I was congratulating him on the financial success of the play which now seemed to be settling down to a long and profitable run. I asked him did he think it would transfer to London—the litmus test of a play's profitability by Dublin theatrical standards—and he almost spluttered back at me, ' Of course it will go to London, why the hell wouldn't it go to London?' ' In that case,' I replied, ' a few of us must at least go over for the first night.' ' A few of us?' he asked incredulously. ' We'll charter a whole bloody plane! There must be enough sports-kings left in Dublin to fill a plane.' ' Sports-king ' was an echo of Dublin small talk, nineteen-thirty vintage—the nearest contemporary expression would

Richard (Dickie) Wyeman, a parson of exquisite sensibilities, an Anglican version of Jim Leathers. Other tenants dwelt in various crannies in this Gruyère-like structure. Thither would come, most nights, brigades of young intelligentsia, platoons of poets, past and future revolutionaries and armchair republicans and free loaders, whose motto was ' myself alone '. No invitation was required, but a large brown bag of bottled stout was obligatory.

The base of Dickie's wobbly financial structure rested on these bottles. There was a small payment given for them on their return to the publican. It was hardly worth anyone's while to collect this, with the result that hundreds of empty bottles would be left in the catacombs each night by departing revellers. After two or three evenings of accumulated bottlery, Dickie would load up a taxi and make a foray into the pub district where clinking glass could be turned to cash. Thus, he provided himself with a modest income, not to mention nightly diversions.

There one would meet, *inter multos alia* Behan, Kavanagh, Cronin, Hutchinson and the young John Jordan, Gainor and his friend, A.K. O'Donoghue (who was a model for O'Keefe in *The Ginger Man*), and who is still, happily, with us; J.P. Donleavy and his wife Valerie and her brother Michael Heron who was an assistant editor of *Envoy,* and J.K. Hillman, another editorial associate of mine, also a Trinity ' G.I.' who is, at the time of writing, the head of the Jung foundation in Switzerland.

There was a room in the catacombs known as the ' day-and-night ' room. It had no windows and its darkness was stygian. Waking up in it, clockless, a man I knew couldn't decide whether it was day or night, but opted (when he saw the street lights still on) for its being the last minutes before dawn and thus the darkest. He made his way, therefore, towards the local where cheerful illumination proclaimed the pub to be just opened—as he piously thought. He was much chagrined when he found that it was, in fact, just *closing* for the night and he had lost a whole day of his life. He feared the obliteration of further periods of time, so he moved his couch into the corridor, from which draughty retreat he could at least keep an eye on the street and be able to record the tell-tale differences between the diurnal and nocturnal phases of the planet.

Crist himself had a weird sort of solar ' clock ' for keeping him posted on the crucial happenings of the day—such as opening time and the ' holy hour '. He had sheets of cardboard with numbers on them placed in certain parts of the living-room in Newtown Avenue. As the sun rose, it would strike these, through the window, at different, known times. Minute adjustments had to be made each day to allow for the sun's relative position altering according to the seasons. It seemed to serve him well enough, for he was never known to miss opening time in Jack O'Rourke's pub in Blackrock. He knew a thing or two about astronomy and kept a telescope.

The time Behan had got the month for beating up the Trinity porters, previously mentioned, it was I who collected him from Mountjoy. They release you from prison at an unearthly hour, so it was around 7 a.m. when I called. Governor Sean Kavanagh, whom I knew and admired, met me at the front gate and handed Brendan over to me in a touching ceremony. Certain Dublin pubs are licensed to open for early morning workers such as dockers and the markets. Brendan had to be taken to one of these—but fast. As I drove him there, he bowed and waved pudgy fingers at the early pedestrians as if he were the Queen Mother being driven in her landau to Royal Ascot.

When we arrived at our destination in Capel Street, near the fruit and vegetable markets, we found Gainor propping up the counter and exchanging early morning gallantries with one of the ladies of the night. It was a great re-union for all concerned and the conviviality continued until all the pubs were legitimately opened, when a regular ' crawl ' began.

Everyone knew Brendan, even then, and the fact that he was just out of jail didn't make the slightest difference. ' The dirty, rotten, lousy, English murderers,' one old crone cackled tooth-lessly at him, ' what did they put you in for?' It could have been for raping children for all she knew—or cared.

Frank O'Connor, the celebrated Irish short story writer, once stated in a British newspaper how he was so well known that if you sent a letter to him as ' Frank O'Connor, writer ' and addressed it to the newspaper boy at the bottom of Grafton Street, he would get it. Well, the postman from Grafton Street came to me at *Envoy* with a letter thus addressed. ' Who is Frank O'Connor anyway? ' he asked me. ' The fella at the end of Grafton Street says he never heard of him but that you or that sign writer Brendan Behan might.' Such is fame.

We went to Paris in 1947—the Crists (Gainor, Con and the baby), Tony McInerney, Michael Heron, my sister Oonagh and her husband Alexis Guedroitz. One day, as part of the detest-able grind of rubber-necking our way around the capital, we found ourselves on top of the Eiffel Tower, where Crist intro-duced us to a fellow-American, presumably a friend, though whether the friendship was struck up just then or was of greater antiquity, we did not know. At any rate, I was left with his friend while Gainor and the rest repaired to a handy bar located on the *troisième étage*. At a loss to know what to discuss with a complete stranger, I fell back on predictable small-talk about the view and how uncommonly good it was. My companion seemed unhappy with this turn of the con-versation, shuffling his feet and making doleful grimaces. Afterwards, Crist told me that he was totally blind. It was a pity, he felt, that I had to discourse on the scenery. I mention this only to illustrate the well-known Cristian syndrome, whereby seemingly mundane events took on new and disturb-ing meanings by mere virtue of his presence.

I remember being invited to dine at the Crist residence, 1 Newtown Avenue (which became 1 Mohammed Road in the book). The house has since become a chemist's shop. When I asked, the present occupants admitted to knowing nothing of a ginger man, real or fictitious or, indeed, an author by the name of J.P. Donleavy.

M

My wife recalled that evening better than I did. Some curious kind of meat was frying on the gas stove and emitting blue, toxic fumes when we arrived. Orange boxes had been arranged upon which to set the dinner. The upstairs toilet was broken and effluent was oozing through the ceiling plaster. (Later, the toilet was to come through, narrowly missing a lady who was then much advanced in pregnancy!)

Crist suggested we adjourn to the Three Tunn Inn—that the ladies could call us there when the meal was ready for serving. We departed and, after some time, Con (Mrs Crist), asking my wife to keep an eye on the meat in case it went on fire, also departed for the pub. Finally, the meat *did* go on fire in front of her eyes, whereupon she too decided to join us. And that was the dinner.

At the time of the outbreak of the Korean war, Pearse Hutchinson, in a poem, had predicted *our* destruction. I asked Crist if, in view of this, he had any contingency plans. He said he had given the matter thought. If this war got any bigger than the ' local ' one it still was, he would catch the first ' Aer Fungus ' plane to London. There he would enrol in the US Armed Forces at the embassy in Grosvenor Square. Having served in the Marines in the second world war, he would be bound to be appointed, at least, an NCO. Being the first to enlist, he figured he would, at least, be made a recruiting clerk. ' I intend,' he confided, ' to spend this particular war behind a mahogany flying fortress.'

I never saw ' Crist ', as we called him, again after he left Dublin in the early 'fifties, but he wrote to me from time to time. Once from London he asked me for a reference for a job with an insurance firm. I wonder did he get it? I ask this, knowing that it would have been a worse fate than not getting it. He wrote me a card another time from Madrid, and asked that his love be given to ' D.D.D. ' This cliché description, ' Dear Dirty Dublin', which occurred originally in the journals of Lady Morgan (1783-1859), is applied mainly by provincials, and is not entirely lacking in factual basis.

He died on board a cargo ship returning to the United States in the early 'sixties (presumably of cirrhosis). The duty-free liquor on board ship, after years of the inexpensive wines and spirits of Spain (the country in which, with his second wife, he had eventually made his domicile) proved fatal. He was buried in Teneriffe—the US consul reading the service as the ship paused in mid-Atlantic at this venue rather than conducting the customary burial at sea. It is said that the captain, who had become a boozing companion of Gainor on the trip, very nearly had to join him in this corner of a foreign field which is now forever a unique Irish-American literary landmark, but somehow escaped this distinction: the nearest he got to it was to have been carried down the gang-plank on a stretcher, in an advanced condition of D.T.'s, behind the Gingerman's coffin.

What was it he had? What charisma was his who never even *attempted* to do anything, let alone complete it, said nothing memorable, yet whose memory is so much cherished; that caused society to somehow spin about *him;* that made two women love and marry him, penniless and alcoholic though he was, and a man write a book and a play about him that has caused a near-cult throughout the world? Was he simply a *succès de scandale*?

I don't know. He was the subject and not the creator of art, but an indefatigable bohemian and, of all those friends of mine from that time, he is the one I would most dearly like to summon from the shades, for the specific purpose of renewing one night of his exceptional company in the Dublin he knew so well and, as his card tells us, loved. Happily, for future generations, he was the catalyst that Donleavy needed to commemorate Dublin in those years, and surely nobody has done it better?

13

Remembering How We Stood

Someone should go to the door;
Perhaps time wished to apologise
For taking off with all our days.

Padraig J. Daly: *Someone Should*

During the 'Emergency'—how long it seems in retrospect
but how short it was in fact—and for the years immediately
following it I lived with my mother and family in Stillorgan,
only seven miles from the centre of the city but open countryside then. Our specific area was near Leopardstown racecourse
and 'Boss' Croker's house which is now the residence of the
British Ambassador. Boss Croker had ruled Tammany Hall
when it was the Irish Mafia that controlled New York in the
early years of this century. In the grounds of 'Glencairn' his
Derby winner *Orby* lies buried. When *Orby* returned to Ireland
he was met by torchlight processions and brass bands—for he
was a hundred-to-one against and the 'Boss' had put on a
pound for each and every one of his retainers. It was said that
no one in Sandyford drew a sober breath for at least three
months.

Our home was Burton Hall. It was a modest enough 'hall'
even though it had been built by members of the Guinness
family many years ago, but it had splendid gardens and just
enough land attached to it to make farming uneconomical.
Despite this we cultivated its hundred odd acres throughout
the emergency. When the Hitlerian campaigns at last came to
an end and we were no longer dependent on the old Harcourt
Street-Bray railway for our daily forays into the city (motor cars
had returned) many of my friends would visit us for weekends

or evenings and not a few returning ' bonafide ' revellers would take us in as a last port of call before finally calling it a night.

But in early childhood, faraway times long before this chronicle commences, I lived in a large red-bricked house in the hushed calm of Rathgar. This whole area is maturely Victorian in style and has great beauty in certain moods and lights. The origin of this beauty may be found in the harmonious and fitting balance of house to road, architrave to window line, mass to space. Over it all a remote sadness seems to hover, as in a Canaletto painting. The brick, of which it is mostly made, has taken on, with time, the property of light pink sandstone. The monkey-puzzle trees, the weeping willows, have grown old serenely but the soil in the flower-beds has only grown black—from a century of soot, the output of innumerable chimneys.

Roads here seem to end in mountains, and it appears to be not the streets and houses that are thrusting towards the country, but the hills (like earthy glaciers) that are seeping inexorably back into the genteel mellowed suburb. The whole area, including Brighton Square West, where Joyce was born, may, arguably, be the most perfectly intact, homogeneous, early Victorian, urban landscape we have. The architecture is chaste and nearer the Prince Regent than the Prince Consort; for the hand of the Dublin tradesman and master builder (recalling earlier and better disciplines), could not readily fashion things that were alien both to taste and eye. They were men with, perhaps, memories of their own fathers creating Mountjoy and Merrion Squares and, therefore, well-grounded in the canon of the Georgian aesthetic.

Our house was on Orwell Road, which begins at the intersection of Rathgar Avenue and Rathgar Road, the latter a truly noble thoroughfare, graciously wide, running like a lofty geometric statement, through a charming chance medley of structures great and small—until it runs out of ideas and just allows itself to be swallowed by a confusion of lesser, meaner roads and streets.

In ' getting away from it all ', Orwell Road succeeds where its neighbour fails. Starting with two columns of houses at attention and facing each other, it swoops to kiss the despondent Dodder River, before soaring upward and outward for the freedom of the hills, which it eventually finds, becoming en route a delightful meandering country lane. It starts in *Urbs* and ends in *Rus*.

For me, there is a melancholy atmosphere in the area and in the big, sad house where my father died before he was forty, and I was seven—one of the eight children he had left behind him.

In the evenings, when the setting sun lays long shafts of fading gold between the buildings, and the mountains are the first to draw around them the dark clouds of night, the place seems to be carved from rose-coloured alabaster and to be lit ethereally—the whole the creation of some lost race of men. Then it suggests the memory of the vanished Victorian scene; for this Dublin, which belonged to Joyce's father and his contemporaries, seems to be haunted by their spirits.

There were, even in my time, old people there who belonged, very nearly, to that era. I remember Sergeant Sullivan lived on our road—he was the last Sergeant-at-Law appointed and had been on the defence team for Sir Roger Casement at the forlorn ' trial ' in 1916. Old age seemed to have soured him in the end for he would (in his doting crankiness) turn nasty on the memory of Casement himself.

Colonel Dan Broy, one of Michael Collins' spies in Dublin Castle, and later one of the first Commissioners of the Gárda Síochána, lived next door to us. His men were known as the ' Broy Harriers ', and much hated by the IRA. There was an armed guard on his house at all times which, being umbilically attached to ours, more or less put our dwelling under this questionable protection too.

It was to this house and place I returned, after an absence of many years, to live in for the later, unhappier part of the period I have here attempted to recall. Here in the late 'fifties I first realized how time was running on; how the new age

was growing old, and how the people who characterized it
were becoming tired. We were moving into the twilight of a
creative time and the dying days of what could be yet called
a 'movement'. It was a movement without a manifesto, but
it obeyed some inner injunction (or code) which gave it
something suggestive of direction and aim.

There we gave the usual parties over the years, and many
friends came. Indeed, everyone who has been mentioned in
these pages sat around the fire in Rockdale some time or
another, once upon a time. At one of those evenings a journalist, for those bleak, personal reasons that some people nurture,
decided to be more unkind than usual to Paddy Kavanagh.

' You are nothing only a minor poet, Kavanagh,' he rasped.

A lengthy pause.

' Since Homer, *we all are,*' the poet quietly rejoined. It
was Swiftian; it was a reply that might have emanated from
the clouds on Parnassus itself. That Augustan statement
delivered, the journalist quit fooling around with his betters
and betook himself to another place.

After Homer, after Shakespeare . . . and who shall say that
after Kavanagh himself all are not minor poets? But
sufficient pedants will spring forth from the loins of posterity to argue his intention and measure his worth without our
wearying ourselves by giving tongue as well.

He was a great poet, but more important, the last authentic
pastoral voice to produce great poetry. His country world
died in his own days. The rural community is no longer a
separate entity with its own distinctive life-style, even in
Ireland; just another part of the urban sprawl—the part that
manufactures the edibles for the supermarkets. He was a poet
and a peasant but too many of his literary contemporaries
merely wished him to be the latter.

The dung and mud on his boots and fingers were not those
of affectation but of actuality. He was the last poet to work
from the enormous reserves of experience that the encaged,
brutalizing, backbreaking, emasculating toil of the small
farmer provides; for he was composing, not only from the

experience of contemporary man at his humblest level, but reaching backward into pre-history, and feeling instinctively as half-primordial man, newly arrived at the age of enlightenment. Of twentieth-century poets, he was the one who least had to counterfeit a ' pure ' proletarian background; this, in turn, absolved him from the necessity of having to attitudinize vulgarly or strike popularist poses—the big hang-up of the middle-class poets (and weren't they all?) of the mid-century.

The man I knew had a very thin veneer of urbanity—but a great store of wisdom and experience. I believe his quality as a poet was only equalled by his ability to teach. After him, no one should be in doubt as to what poetry is about, or be afraid to set it in motion; but one might as well try, in painting, to emulate the shrieking encapsulated cardinals of Francis Bacon, without having endured his experience, as to reproduce Kavanagh's divine discontent without having lived his life.

Much of the prose writing he has left behind deals with the subject of writing honestly—for he held that great art was truth memorably expressed—believing that all else would follow; form and style would attach to a great thought at the moment of conception and grow mysteriously with it.

To know the earlier pre-Baggotonian man, the man who had, for instance, the intense devotion of a Catholic peasant for the Blessed Virgin, one must read Kavanagh's *The Green Fool,* from which this is but one example:

I was a fatalist drifting inconsequently on the winds of chance, and did not care where they blew me. Only this, I had deep faith in Her that guides the wanderers, and as the boat swayed in the choppy Irish sea, I remembered Her who was litanied Star of the Sea.

What a moat of irreconcilability stood between the personalities of Kavanagh and Behan; how they would exude hostility, each for each, trembling with alienation, yet Kavanagh wrote:

I'm a night-coward and full of tremulous faith in uncanny things.

while Brendan confided to me (and probably to many more):

I am a daylight atheist.

Were they worlds apart? Brendan, the ghetto offspring of teeming slum-ridden, O'Casey Dublin, and Patrick, the child of the rural slum, where you'd wait for a hen to lay an egg to make up the necessary dozen to sell so as to buy a quarter pound of tea?

The hatred they professed for each other is legendary but must not be confused with the real loathing people sometimes share, but rather to prima donnas *engagé*. Writers and artists are endemically quarrelsome; their occupation makes them more distraught and susceptible to hysteria than other professionals; because of art's insecurity and the wounds that the morbidly intelligent inflict upon themselves.

Even Tennyson wearied of poets and their squabbles:

Ah God! the petty fools of rhyme,
That shriek and sweat in pigmy wars.

So we must not think it too great a wonder that in our day and narrower confines they still snap at each other.

'Fame is the spur', and much more so than money. Kavanagh would not have admitted it, but he was well aware that what he had achieved was greater, though less tangible, than that of Brendan who had made the Great White Way. The real poetic prize is the praise of those, whom, at the time you believe to be your peers; as Sir Walter Scott puts it in 'The Lay of the Last Minstrel':

For ne'er
Was Flattery lost on poet's ear;
A simple race! they waste their toil,
For the vain tribute of a smile.

Paddy, it is true, complained endlessly about being unable to make money, or even make friends with monied people, while

Brendan, who had made it, and lots, was genuinely hag-ridden by financial worries right up to his death. He was being badgered fairly relentlessly by the Revenue Commissioners and, like all people who were once poor, allowed the matter of debts to weigh inordinately heavily upon his mind. This was, no doubt, a legacy of pawning days when not to pay the debt meant the loss of something much more valuable, and where even more drastic visitations than appearing in *Stubb's Gazette* awaited the non-payer from the local moneylender or street bookmaker.

In a sense then, they both got what they wanted. The one—raucous, klieg-lit notoriety and short-lived money-to-burn with all its concomitant anxieties. The other—the private esteem of the poetic greats; the quiet background murmur of mandarin approval and the nodding fellowship with the beautiful people, from whom just enough money rubbed off to make life tolerable but not enough to make it exacting.

Myles, that figment, as I have said, of his own imagination, was the greatest comic genius we ever produced, but beneath a plentiful, fertile topsoil of wit lay a stratum of sorrow which, like the limestone beneath the turf of Tipperary, provides the essential ingredient for growth.

He approved, seeing the same quality in Joyce's work, and commented:

> Humour, the handmaid of sorrow and fear, creeps out end-lessly in all Joyce's works. He uses the thing in the same way as Shakespeare does but less formally, to attenuate the fear of those who have belief and who genuinely think that they will be in hell or in heaven shortly, and possibly very shortly. With laughs he palliates the sense of doom that is the heritage of the Irish Catholic. True humour needs this background urgency: Rabelais is funny, but his stuff cloys. His stuff lacks tragedy.

It is a better summary of his own literary self-tragedy than of Joyce.

It is said that he never quite overcame the disappointment when his second novel *The Third Policeman* was rejected by his publishers. His first work *At Swim-Two-Birds* was accepted at once because the reader happened to be Graham Greene who was quick to recognize him as a unique and gifted writer.

Unfortunately, publication coincided with the outbreak of the war in 1939 and what would have been, at another time, a spectacular launching, was utterly obscured by the smoke-screens of polemic and propaganda that then prevailed.

He expected, at least, the same enthusiastic treatment when submitting his *The Third Policeman* but, unfortunately, Greene had left by this time, and a lesser reader churlishly refused his small masterpiece. I have heard it argued that he deliberately put the book out of his head and even succeeded, physically as well as psychologically, in 'losing' it.

Vague rumours that the work lay about somewhere persisted. At least one writer, Niall Sheridan, had read it and helped at Myles' request to edit some of the text. But it never saw the light of day until some years after his death, when it was 'found' and duly published by McGibbon and Kee.

What does seem certain is that his book *The Dalkey Archive* is a version of this work as he *remembered* the text thirty years afterwards. It scarcely bears comparison with the earlier work.

The hiatus which this created in his spiritual progress was never to be remedied. He drove on one flat tyre from then onward. It is the true indication of his heroic qualities that he brought us through all those years laughing despite his own increasing tragedies. The true comic genius can never switch the current off.

He may have felt even more keenly that his work in the Irish language was never seen for its real worth. His translations from the early Irish poets, for instance, are easily as good as Frank O'Connor's, but few were prepared to accord him the distinction of being something of a poet as well as a funny man.

While others were busily interring Irish as a 'dead' language like Latin, intending it to be preserved for their own exclusive necrophilic use, he, by lampooning the Gaels in their own language, was injecting life into it through wit, culture and the sophistication of a mature intelligence. Nothing did more to awaken interest in the language at the time than his novel *An Béal Bocht* (The Poor Mouth).

Where piety and the most restricted nationalism had previously been evoked hopefully to bring the young flocking to the cause of preserving the language, he brought gaiety and satire. They (the others) would have preserved it—in formaldehyde; he would have ' brought it round ' by pouring the wine of wit between its teeth.

I told him once of how, when I was discussing this with Liam O'Flaherty, another master of the Irish language (as well as the English), we had both agreed that the Gaelic League had been a baneful influence on the revival of Irish; that nothing promulgated by old pedants, obsessed with the fear of sex and beauty, and clad in crumpled navy suits festooned with nasty little emblems and watch chains with hurling medals, and spitting words uncouthly through neglected teeth, could ever attract youth. The word ' square ' had not evolved then but we both knew that it was this syndrome that we were discussing; that it was the unfailing role of the anti-artist to take over control of movements born of cultural faith, and eventually smother them.

Had there been more men of his calibre (and indeed women too—for would not a few ravishing blondes and brunettes have been a happy and wholesome incentive?) people with laughter in their hearts as well as wisdom in their heads, in the earlier years when the pietistic chauvinists were beginning to take over, the hope for the survival of Irish as a living language would not be so much in doubt as it now is.

For all these disappointments, Myles was a happy enough man. Of the three writers I have dealt with in these pages at some length, he was the best adjusted to the life that was going on about him yet he was the least ' arty '. He was meticulous and correct. He did not believe that being an author conferred the privileges of being rude and offensive to others not of that calling. He expected the ordinary respect that is the right of any honest burgess.

Shortly before his death, he showed me a receipt from the municipal rates office in respect of the valuation of his house. He asked me if I could spot anything wrong with it. Rates are payable twice-yearly—in January and June. It was now December—and so I observed to my considerable amazement that he was a person who actually paid his rates *in advance*. In fact—and this was the whole point of his disclosure—they had mistakenly dated the receipt a year *further* in advance. His point was that he could, if he so desired, produce it at the appropriate time, and claim that payment was proved to have been made for that year. But I was still much more intrigued by his civic-spirited nature in paying in advance, for the idea of *ever* paying rates, if they could by any manner or means be avoided, would be as alien to Kavanagh or Behan as going on the dry for life.

14

The Swan in the Evening

She stepped away from me and she moved through the fair,
And fondly I watched her go here and go there,
Then she went her way homeward with one star awake,
As the swan in the evening moves over the lake.

Padraic Colum: ' She Moved Through the Fair '

When the idea of putting down these memories became fixed
in my mind there was one more ' death in the family '. It was
the death of a father figure, a poet who had preceded all my
friends here remembered and outlasted them as well. A gentler
bard never existed.

Padraic Colum, in a long and distinguished life devoted to
Irish letters in his capacity of poet, critic and chronicler,
encouraged and befriended more Irish writers than he could
remember. In particular, he and his wife had helped out
James Joyce and the Joyce family for the better part of his life,
not only by the thousand small favours and courtesies of the
faithful friends that they were, but by the more arduous good
deeds of helping out the family in the unceasing rounds of
domestic calamities and illnesses, and the more nerve-racking
labour of applying pressure onto people of influence, or
wheedling money from people of affluence—on Joyce's behalf.
And this, despite the fact that the Colums were themselves
struggling young writers, eking out a scant enough livelihood,
teaching and taking odd jobs. This was a consideration that
would not have greatly troubled the master. Joyce was nobly
served by his friends—in particular, Eugene Jolas, Harriet

Shaw Weaver, Sylvia Beach, Frank Budgeon, John Francis Byrne, W.B. Yeats, Ezra Pound, but above all, Padraic Colum. Of Ezra Pound, Joyce had written in a letter of 1932:

> It is nearly twenty years since he first began his vigorous campaign on my behalf and it is probable that, but for him, I should still be the unknown drudge that he had discovered—if it was a discovery.

But ten years earlier again, Colum had started *his* vigorous campaign, and had been exerting pressure to have *Dubliners* accepted by Maunsel & Roberts in Dublin.

A half-century later, in 1962, when the James Joyce Tower Society was formed, Padraic Colum accepted the position of president. Our purpose, as I have mentioned, was to make the old Martello Tower in Sandycove a Joyce museum and library. We held our fortnightly committee meetings on the fourth floor of the Bailey.

Colum, who was then but a sprightly eighty-one-year-old, used to bound up the stairs two at a time, well ahead of the entire breathless committee; many of them were half his age. As president, he felt it was his duty to be seated and in command of the proceedings before the rest, but also to be in a position to welcome them as his guests. Someone somewhere has described a camel as a horse designed by a committee. More akin to Hydra, the nine-headed serpent (with the in-built ability to grow two further heads for each one severed) than a camel, we tended to head out in a dozen different directions in pursuit of Joyce's mast and, indeed, would often have done so but for his gentle but quite insistently restraining hand.

It was his practicality that most impressed us—*he* was the one concerned with the apparent trivia, the minutiae, while we dispensed clouds of well-meant waffle. That the Tower Museum came into being and got off to a good start at all was in large measure thanks to his good-will and patience—gifts that were now, in old age, serving the posthumous Joyce of scholar and thesis-writer as they had once served, so timely, the harassed, improvident and beleagured Joyce of Colum's hard-pressed youth and middle-age.

It was 18 January 1972, and a bulky, streamlined liver-coloured plastic casket lay on its catafalque before the high altar of the Church of the Holy Name in Ranelagh, having been flown in from New York the previous evening. This massive sarcophagus contained the elfin remains of Padraic Colum, last survivor of the Irish literary renaissance; final flicker of the Celtic twilight.

As the Requiem Mass proceeded, thoughts turned, not un-naturally, to the occupant of that ungainly coffin; not only to the seventy odd years of mainly literary endeavour which his active life embraced, but the truly daunting gap, as expressed in terms of ideas and aspirations, that lay between the now and the beginnings, and which only this frail body had eventually spanned.

Seventy years earlier, Colum was one of the young lions AE had marked down for great things in the Dublin literary scene presided over by Yeats, Lady Gregory and, to no small extent, the former editor of the *Dublin Magazine*, Seumas O'Sullivan. Joyce was another hopeful but, although AE applauded what he called ' the perfect art ' of his early poems —one can imagine the way he enunciated that—finding them ' as delicate and dainty as Watteau pictures ' (how did the creator of Molly Bloom's soliloquy respond to that nosegay?) he felt obliged to add that he had much greater confidence in another of his young men, namely, the up-and-coming Padraic Colum.

Below the bleak brow of Shelmartin, itself crouching in the lee of Ben Edair, or Howth Head, to give the name its later Scandinavian modification, is a small cemetery—an annexe to the overcrowded one facing the sea at Kilbarrack that Brendan Behan once described as ' the healthiest grave-yard in Ireland '. Here, Padraic Colum's wife, Mary, also rests. Icy rain fell on bare heads that numbing funeral morning. Five thrushes huddled into themselves on an over-hanging bough—watching. Out in Dublin bay, an old rust-bucket of a coaster laboured through melodramatic seas as a harsh south-easterly sent porter-foam scudding before it. About the open mouth of the double vault rose hillocks of freshly-mined umberous clay. Father Gunnings, on the crest of the grave, said the prayers for the dead and recited a decade of the rosary.

And then there came a benediction.

Benedict Kiely stood up and spoke words, lyrical and humane, about his friend. It was possible then, for the first time that day, to appreciate that it was a man that resided at the core of this ritual and not simply an entry in the *Dictionary of National Biography*, or the *Encyclopaedia Britannica*, under the heading: Colum, P., (Irish). Poet. 1881-1972.

The last words spoken were those of Edmund Krochalis of Newhaven, Connecticut, a friend of the deceased. He, in turn, read a message from Micheál MacLiammóir, which ended with the line, ' may the wild earth that covers his body lie lightly over him.'

Time's clay lies heavily on those who are even moderately famous; despite all supplications, posterity will come, inquisitively and, of course, irreverently, to rake forsaken memories, open old graves; only the souls of those who never vainly claimed greatness or rashly aspired to immortality can truly be said to rest in peace.

I looked at all that sodden slurry and wondered . . .

Index